RITE OF PASSAGE

TALES OF BACKPACKING 'ROUND EUROPE

D0951278

LONELY PLANET PUBLICATIONS
Melbourne • Oakland • London • Paris

Rite of Passage: Tales of Backpacking 'Round Europe

Published by Lonely Planet Publications

Head Office:
90 Maribyrnong Street, Footscray, Vic 3011, Australia
Locked Bag 1, Footscray, Vic 3011, Australia

Branches:
150 Linden Street, Oakland CA 94607, USA
10a Spring Place, London NW5 3BH, UK
1 rue Dahomey, 75011, Paris, France

Published 2003
Printed by The Bookmaker International Ltd
Printed in China

Copy-edited by Meaghan Amor and Janet Austin
Designed by Daniel New
Layout by Gerilyn Attebery
Map by Tony Fankhauser

National Library of Australia Cataloguing-in-Publication entry

Rite of passage: tales of backpacking 'round Europe.

ISBN 1 74059 593 9.

1. Backpacking - Europe - Anecdotes. 2. Travelers'
writings. 3. Europe - Description and travel. I. Johnson,
Lisa, 1970-. (Series: Lonely Planet journeys).

914.0456

For Izzy

CONTENTS

MAP   VI

INTRODUCTION   IX

CHAPTER 1: GETTING THE HANG OF IT   1

First-timer – Thorn Tree   2
City of Poets – Will Bradshaw in Spain   5
The Other Menu – Valerie Pehrson in Amsterdam   11
The Quest – Karen Lee Boren in London   17
Walk on by – Thorn Tree   22
The Professional – Lisa Johnson in Hungary   24
Night Passage – Gail Cochrane in the English Channel   28
Finnish Saunas: The Naked Truth – Dave Fox in Finland   30
Waking up to Winter – John Morgan in Rome   33
Taken In – Tom Smith in France   40
Retsina Road – Harry Rolnick in Greece   44
Can You Find the Flusher – Roberta Beach Jacobson
in Germany   47

CHAPTER 2: YOU GET WHAT YOU PAY FOR   49

Be warned! – Thorn Tree   50
One More Story to Tell – Katherine Jamieson in Prague   51
The Delinquents of Málaga – William Sutton in Spain   56
At Least You Have a Seat – Myrna McKee in France   62
My Stinky Cheese Night – Kathy Coudle King in Amsterdam   66
Fierce Hospitality – Dani Valent in Turkey   70
Slow Bus to Fethiye – Liza Perrat in Turkey   71
Saints' Station, Barcelona – Will Bradshaw in Spain   74
This Isn't the Greyhound, Is It? – Jim Eagen in Prague   78
Sleeping with Hercules – Tara Kolden in Corfu   83

CHAPTER 3: GETTING IT ON   87

Has this ever happened to you? – Thorn Tree   88
Fortress – Lisa K. Buchanan in Corfu   91
The Love of Strangers – Diana Omo Evans in Paris   96
A Fine Italian Hand – Carol Schwalberg in Italy   101
And I Loved a Soldier – David-Matthew Barnes in Greece   103
French Speakeasy – Mo Fleming in Paris   105
The Little Mother – Ryan Forsythe in Prague   107
Sailing – Lisa Guest in Greece   112
Epiphany – Ginu Kamani in Greece   114
Doubting Tamas – R. Ilayne in Hungary   117
Inside the Cherries – Sandra Dorr in Italy   124
Prose of Paris – Sarah Goodwin in Paris   127
The Paris debate – Thorn Tree   129
Caffe Superman – Lynn Schmeidler in Florence   130

CHAPTER 4: BEING THERE   135

Where do you learn the most? – Thorn Tree   136
Naked Hippies and Bonfires – Lori Horvitz in Istanbul   138
Mary McGregor – Lisa Beatman in Ireland   142
A Longing for Union – Mary Ann Larkin in Bulgaria   144
Dancing Italian – Marjorie Maddox in Venice   151
A Slight Leaning Backward – Greg Tuleja in Paris   153
Nocturnal Madrileños – Marshall Krantz in Madrid   158
Might as Well Take It – Lisa Johnson in Amsterdam   163
Paros – Helen Ellis in Greece   168
Balkan Fragments: Gypsy – Karen Lehmann in Yugoslavia   171
Walter – Jennifer Spiegel in Russia   174
After a Month in Germany – Aviya Kushner in Germany   178
Pink Dress – Lorna Smedman in Florence   181
The Other Shore – Brent Olson in Italy   187
Home sweet home . . . Arrgghh! – Thorn Tree   192

ACKNOWLEDGMENTS   199

INTRODUCTION

The plan was simple, standard and time-honored. After graduating from high school we would pack up our bags, leaving behind that terrifying world of Darwinian social competition and putting to rest permanently all our haunting feelings of self-doubt or inadequacy. Europe beckoned, drawing us with its history, its rich and artistic cultures, its dramatic and varied landscapes, and its relaxed drinking laws. Best of all, though, was the promise of *freedom*. We were Adults, dammit, and this was going to be our break-out trip. No one in Europe was aware of just what total dorks we actually were. As far as those crazy Europeans knew, we were charming, alluring adventurers from a faraway place, come to taste the local culture and perhaps break a few hearts before moving on to the next port of call.

Sadly, the plan began to unravel all too soon. The first indication came on the train through Germany, where I noticed that we were surrounded by Beautiful People – smooth, slick and dressed to the nines. Meanwhile, my friends and I had made vast strides in the Hairiness and Pervasive Body Odor departments. "No suave, sophisticated voyagers we," I thought, "but at least we have our quick wits, cosmopolitan air, and travelers' savvy about us." That was before we headed to Scotland and spent half a day wandering the streets of Inverness (not the world's most befuddling metropolis by any standard), lost. Finally, we swallowed our pride and asked a passing constable for directions. "Excuse me, sir, do you know where High Street is?" The look he gave us was a mordant mixture of contempt, amusement and impatience. "Aye," he responded, and pointed his stick at the sign directly over his head, which identified the road we had been wandering on for hours as High Street. We fumbled through countless other episodes of this nature as we made our way across Europe. Gradually, it began to dawn on me that I was not the mature, world-weary traveler that I had hoped; there was still a lot of that geeky schoolkid left in me. Much more than I would care to admit.

Since that eye-opening trip, I've returned to Europe many a time, both for "pleasure" (there's a little masochism in all of us) and as a travel writer. I've gazed over the Urals, danced till dawn in Madrid, and lived the "alternative" life in Copenhagen and Amsterdam. I've made friends and enemies from Marrakesh to Moscow. I don't know if I've broken any hearts, but I've certainly had mine broken countless times (often on a frighteningly regular basis). And it has gotten no better. The people of Europe have seen through my facade and recognized my naïveté and general clue-lessness every single time. Some of them happily accept that I cannot speak their language or find my way to the train station, while others are less forgiving. But to this day, they haven't once fallen for my Experienced Traveler routine.

It is for this reason that I was delighted when the Powers That Be at Lonely Planet brought to me the anthology of stories that you're holding in your hand. I had just come off an exhausting stint as the coordinating author of Lonely Planet's *Europe on a Shoestring*, wherein my colleagues and I did our best to cram every indispensable fact about an entire continent into one book. *Europe on a Shoestring* tries hard to be an amiable companion, cracking jokes now and then and sharing a few stories along the way. But at its core, it's a hard-nosed little bugger, concerned with the building blocks of travel: bus schedules, accommodation prices, how likely it is that the food in a particular restaurant will kill you, etc. Important stuff, doubtless, and just what you need when you are preparing for a trip or are actually on the road. But it's hardly the stuff of dreams – at least, the dreams of a prospective first-time traveler to the Continent. And that's where this book comes in.

Rite of Passage is as much about reality as *Europe on a Shoestring* is, but it's about that side of reality that makes the other side (you know, the one full of climate charts and customs lists and ticket collectors) worth experiencing. The way I see it, *Rite of Passage* is almost the mirror image of *Europe on a Shoestring.* Whereas the latter presents the hard information in as digestible a format as possible, the former conveys the sweetness, glory, frustration and despair of traveling in Europe in an entirely different format. This is it: Europe and You, with none of the day-to-day minutiae getting in the way. To underscore the raw sincerity of the short stories in this anthology, the editor, Lisa Johnson, has included conversations among travelers on the Thorn Tree (http://thorntree.lonelyplanet.com) – Lonely Planet's online travel forum, which serves as a repository of "insider" information for travelers. The end result is a fresh, original assortment of tales that occasionally comes across as naïve, uninformed or even a little rough around the edges. And that's perfect. Because while we'd like to think of Europe as a land where the buses run on time (in the majority of places), where the food won't kill you (for the most part) and where travelers are a common phenomenon and well taken care of, the truth is that first-time travel to Europe can be as harrowing, tumultuous and uplifting as just about anything. There's a reason that they call it a "life-changing experience."

With this in mind, *Rite of Passage* has been put together strategically, presenting the travel experience as chronologically as possible. The first chapter, "Getting the Hang of It," deals with the awkward, stammering introduction to a place that so often constitutes a first encounter with Europe. Will Bradshaw, in "City of Poets," demonstrates that being able to roll with the punches is the key to enjoying a destination, no matter how romanticized one's notion of it; while Lisa Johnson's "The Professional" reveals that all the qualifications, planning and moral weight in the world may not be able to overcome an old woman's sense of propriety. The chapter explores the quandaries likely to befall the first-time traveler, whether they deal with matters of tradition and hospitality, or slightly more mundane – but no less crucial – questions, such as the dilemma posed by Roberta Beach Jacobson: "Can You Find the Flusher?"

Just when you think you're in the groove, the real problems start. In the second chapter, "You Get What You Pay For," writers wrestle with the inconveniences, stresses and feelings of impotence engendered by getting ripped off or cheated. No one can help but cringe as they read about William Sutton being robbed by his new-found "friends" in "The Delinquents of Málaga," or remain unmoved by Will Bradshaw's story of trustingly (and gullibly) leaving his bags in the care of a stranger in "Saints' Station, Barcelona." Lest you think that Spain is the only place where hapless visitors are at risk, Liza Perrat reveals the details of a long journey through Turkey in "Slow Bus to Fethiye," while Kathy Coudle King details her "Stinky Cheese Night" in Amsterdam. With any luck, those fortunate enough to read these stories will travel with their ears pricked up and eyes wide open.

But it isn't all bad, and in fact it's sometimes mind-blowingly good. After all, Europe is the land of romance, and it still speaks the language of love. The Continent, and its denizens, prove irresistible to the authors of the third chapter, all of whom know how to light that ephemeral spark. In Paris, *amour*-central itself, Diana Omo Evans discovers "The Love of Strangers," while Lisa K. Buchanan builds her own personal "Fortress" to protect her heart in Greece. Sandra Dorr finds romance while making her way by ship to Italy in "Inside the Cherries"; farther north in the same country, Lynn Schmeidler learns about true anguish while waiting for her hero at "Caffe Superman."

In the end, the whole experience comes down to two things: how travel affects the self, and how it touches others in the world. The final chapter, "Being There," explores the profound effects of travel on the traveler and those they meet along the way. Lisa Beatman captures something quintessential about the Irish spirit in "Mary McGregor," while in Bulgaria Mary Ann Larkin experiences "A Longing for Union" when she meets and discovers a profound connection with a group of bohemian poets and artists. In "Walter," Jennifer Spiegel ruminates on how one instant, one action, can touch two people's lives. And in Italy, Brent Olson ponders how well two people can ever really know each other, in his story "The Other Shore." And, in case you were wondering what happens when it's all over, the denizens of the Thorn Tree offer some theories of their own in "Home Sweet Home . . . Arrgghh!"

And finally, it's only fair to offer a word of warning. These stories were not written by veterans of European travel. Quite possibly a hardened voyager may throw up their hands and cry, "That's not right. Prague is *nothing like that!*" or something to that effect. And that's fine. Each city, each village, each hill in Europe presents a different facet to different people. Your experience will be your own, and once you've shaped it, it will forever color your view of a place and a time. No matter how many times I return to London, I still remember it as "the city where it snows in early December"; and every time I picture London, I see it through a blanket of whiteness. These authors have captured instances and images that will differ drastically from yours in the particulars, but will agree in spirit with what you shall encounter. The veterans have written their own stories already, and the details have been filled in. That's not to say that if you're an experienced traveler, you'll get nothing out of this book. But you'll probably have to fight the urge to "correct" the stories, to make them fit with what you know.

I hope that these tales inspire you, move you, entertain you . . . all the things that good stories are supposed to do. But I hope more than anything else that these stories *excite* you, so that you'll be champing at the bit. Europe is out there, and it's waiting for you. Remember: if they like me over there, they'll *love* you. Hell, I love you already, just for reading all the way to the end of this introduction.

Now get on with it! Don't you have places to go?

Vivek Waglé, coordinating author *Europe on a Shoestring*

CHAPTER 1

GETTING THE HANG OF IT

cbmh
(3 replies)

first-timer . . . help me . . .

ok, so i have bought my ticket and it's only a month until i go to brussels . . . i'm scared shitless . . . i'm going by myself, i've never traveled before. two mates of mine who were gonna travel with me bailed 'cos they spent too much of their savings on, um, stuff . . . they reckon they'll make it in a few more months, but i'll believe that when i see it . . .

i know a guy in brussels and people in dublin, but i don't wanna seem like a leech . . . i have heaps of money, well, aussie dollars anyways . . . so half that in euros . . . i just have absolutely no idea what the fudge i'm doing . . . but as neil finn said (or was it tim?), "better to jump than hesitate, i need a change and i can't wait."

um, anyone got any advice, tips, places i shouldn't miss . . . or anyone as clueless as me lookin' for some safety in numbers??

it's a strange feeling, the combination of excitement and sheer terror . . .

RoadWarrior
1.

Don't worry

It's not difficult, no reason to be concerned. You'll find many solo travelers, you will definitely not be the only one.

You could be in for a bit of culture shock, although it's quite manageable. I would do this before you go:

- If you speak a bit of a European language, start practicing it. French, Spanish and German are all

175% Page:

useful, and not just in their home countries. Your trip will go more easily if you accept the notion of learning some of these.

- Make a point of trying to embrace new things. Leave the Vegemite at home, and go local – you traveled a long way, so you may as well adjust.

- Bring a few things from home – music you like, photos, souvenirs, etc. Not only will that help you to cope, but the people you meet will be curious to learn more about you. Pictures of your friends, family, pets, home, etc., can help to do that.

- If you like to keep a journal, bring one with you. If you can play an instrument reasonably well, and it's not too bulky, you might wish to bring that, too. You could be the night's entertainment at your hostel, and it makes it easier to meet people.

Good luck and have fun.

---

gawkabout
2.

best mates

Best travel buddies are the ones that bail at the last minute: after you've bought your ticket. It makes ya go anyway.

Strangers are more likely to chat with a lone traveler.

Don't worry. Just accept things are different. That's why they call us "yank whiners." We comment on our comfort zone vs. the real world.

Trains are a great way to travel. It gives you quality time with folk. We all learn from each other.

Raeanne
3.

I was in the same boat!

Hey there . . . don't worry! I went to Europe for ten months and traveled by myself. I had never traveled before. Just go for it and be strong. Go there to have the time of your life. Just be careful, but make sure you have fun!

Take care!

WILL BRADSHAW, A TEACHER AND
FREELANCE WRITER, HAS MADE TWO
TRIPS TO EUROPE. HE IS CURRENTLY
A GRADUATE STUDENT AT MIT STUDY-
ING URBAN PLANNING AND REAL
ESTATE DEVELOPMENT.

CITY OF POETS
WILL BRADSHAW

I want to be nice, but the sardines push me over the edge. I think it's the sucking that gets to me the most. The long forceful slurps, like he has no hands and has to make the fish jump the gap between his mouth and plate. Either that or the growing pile of severed heads with buggy fish eyes staring at me. I make a pact with myself. He will not ruin my Granada. Tomorrow I will wake early and chase the poetry of these streets without him.

In Granada, even the names of hostels are poetry. My room, number 206, is in a hostel on the Alhambra hill: "El agua es como la luz" ("The Water is Like Light"). Seven years before, I had discovered Lorca, and was hooked. Now, after two days with nothing but *pensamientos* (thoughts) to sustain me, I have arrived in this city of my dreams. This time, it will be me floating through the Albayzín watching the Alhambra glow red on the hill above me, sipping Spanish beer while gypsy music enfolds me in its rhythms.

Arriving at the hostel, I enter my room, then stop. On the far bed, a furry pile of a man is sweating in his underwear. A tangle of hair connects loosely to the top of his head, but could hurl off in a hundred different directions at a moment's notice. Running down the left lens of his glasses is a large fissure, threatening but never quite splitting it in two.

"*Salud*," he says.

SPAIN

5

"*Salud*," I repeat. "I am sharing the room with you tonight."

"*Bon, bon,*" he mumbles, while fumbling around and rearranging the possessions on his bed. "Your bed, no?" He points to the unmade bed where he is not sitting.

I nod.

"*Bon, bon*. Your sheets, no?" He hands me a pile of neatly folded, starched white linen.

"*Merci.*" I place the linen on a chair, and start to make up my bed.

"Yes, tonight is very good. I am French."

"Yes, I can tell. Where are you from?"

"France."

"Yes, I know you are from France."

"Yes."

"Where in France?"

He looks at me for a long time, then violently rubs his face and head. Bursts of breath escape as his hand runs back and forth across his nose and mouth, and white flakes of dandruff drift down around him, as though he were trapped in a Christmas globe.

"I speak English only a little."

"*Habla español?*"

He answers in English. "My Spanish is only a little."

"Well, I speak almost no French." I pick up a pillowcase and stuff my pillow into it. "So I guess we're stuck."

He claps his hands together loudly, smiling widely. "Marseille. In France, I am from Marseille."

I nod and toss the pillow onto my bed. Down the corridor, someone says the word, "*Bon.*" In a show of athleticism that belies his roly-poly figure, my roommate leaps onto the floor, keen to find the source of the sound. Everything wiggles, jiggles and shakes: his cheeks, his legs, his jello gut that falls over the waistband of his underwear. Even the bed where he has been sitting jostles back and forth, spilling his haphazard stacks of postcards.

"The person, he is French, no?" I shrug my shoulders. He hesitates a moment, then walks through the door clad only in his underwear. I can hear him rubbing his face as he pounds up and down the corridor.

After about five minutes he returns to the room and stands between our beds, staring at the door. I tap him on the shoulder.

"I am going out to eat." I make a scooping motion with my hand, open my mouth, and pantomime like I am chewing. "Would you like to come?"

"*Bon, bon*. Yes, I would like to eat. I will dress, no?"

"Probably a good idea," I say, and wander into the bathroom.

He puts on brown slacks and a rumpled blue shirt. The collar pokes up in different directions; his shirt is missing a button in the middle where his belly pokes through. The pants are also wrinkled, and about an inch below the top, the zipper is pulled onto the fabric and stuck. A small bit of blue cloth pokes through the hole like a warning flag.

"Ready, no?" He holds his hands up wide.

City of my dreams, Granada. And after all these years, I get this.

"Sure, let's go."

Directly beneath the hostel, the street bends off to the left and starts its zigzagging descent through the forest surrounding the Alhambra, tumbling down to Plaza Nueva at the foot of the hill. Pedestrian traffic follows a more direct route down the hillside. Where the street turns left, steps lead down to a gravel pathway that cuts its way through the trees. Stately trunks mark the edges of the path, and above us, a criss-crossing canopy of branches serves as a backdrop for long, dancing shadows cast by the streetlamps.

I imagine Lorca walking this same pathway years before me, see him stopping to lay back in the gravel while shadows play across his body, envision him writing "Canción Otoñal" beneath this canopy of limbs that roofs the trail. His words reverberate in the wind-rustled leaves.

"What are you doing, the United States?"

Lorca is jarred from my mind. "I don't understand."

My companion rubs at his face nervously. "You are in the United States. What are you doing?"

"Oh, I'm a student. I go to university."

"Yes, yes, I went to university some." He claps his hands just once, exuberantly.

After the clap, he is quiet for a moment. I peer into the woods, but my eyes are unable to penetrate beyond the first grouping of trees. Gazing up into the branches, I am fascinated by the lamp-lit patterns of clarity and blankness, but Lorca doesn't return.

Eventually, an outdoor café comes into view. People in linen suits sit at cloth-covered tables drinking wine from expensive-looking glasses. He heads straight for the menu. I follow a few steps behind.

"Much money," he says as I approach, snapping his fingers against the post where the menu is displayed. People turn around, and the waiters glare. "Is too much no? We should go down to square. More people, less money."

"That's fine. I just need to eat."

"*Bon, bon.* We find food. We find good prices. Is very interesting for me, the prices."

Just below the restaurant, the road meets our path once again. We cross the street, follow a second set of steps, walk past a fountain and round a corner. Our path disappears, and gravel turns to cobblestones. Trees become houses, hotels and shops, pressed too tightly into the road and each other.

The stillness transforms as well. There are people in doorways, standing on porches smoking cigarettes, darting in and out of the many hotels along the street. Behind this activity is the hum of Plaza Nueva, distant enough for individual sounds to blend and twist together like the constant rush of water. Suddenly, I know what Lorca meant when he wrote, "*la canción del agua es una cosa eterna*" ("the song of water is an eternal thing").

"At the plaza, many restaurants will be there, *bon*?"

"*Bon*. What kind of food do you like?"

"I want eat like people here, no."

"Yes, but what? Do you know paella?"

"Paella, yes. *Bon, bon*." He claps and giggles. "We have a paella. And sun-gria. It is vino with the fruit, no?"

"Oh, *sangria*. Yes, it is very good."

"*Bon*." He struts slightly ahead of me, and the street spits us out into the plaza like that – him prancing in front, blue banner of shirt poking through his zipper, me walking behind, awed by the grandeur of it all.

The plaza is filled with people, street bands, couples walking hand in hand, waiters expertly carrying trays through the ever-changing mass of bodies and café tables. An orange-and-white restaurant awning is right in front of us. He shoots towards it, walks right in front of three people already looking at the menu. He snaps his fingers against it. They step back, hold their hands up at chest level in self-defense.

"Paella 650 pesetas. Is good, no?"

"Yes, that's great. You want to eat?"

"No, we must go back in streets. Go small places, *bon*?" He gives one clap, and is off. I follow him to four more restaurant windows, meet the stares of people around us as he snaps his fingers loudly into the menu. Finally, I can't take it anymore.

"I'm going into this restaurant to eat now." I point to make myself clear.

"I join you," he says, sadly. But the maître d' informs us that they have just closed.

"*Bon, bon*. I know a place. Come this way." And he is off again, his confidence restored. He leads us back to a restaurant we'd passed only a few minutes before. It is open, but they are out of paella.

Overcooked chicken and french fries is not the meal I had in mind for my first night in Granada. Across the table from me, my roommate is tearing the heads from sardines and swallowing them whole, every gulp accompanied by a long sucking sound. Periodically, a stream of liquid escapes his lips and runs down his chin.

The next morning I get up while he is still in bed, shower and dress quietly, but my movement wakes him.

"Today, I will come with you. We get a better room some-where."

"No," I lie. "I might leave the city today."

"It is okay. We get a room together tonight. You leave tomorrow."

"No, thanks. I don't want to tie myself down."

We shake hands, and I walk out of the hostel into the streets of Granada, done with him, finally free to search for the poetry I have come to find.

Scrapping my plan to visit the Alhambra, I decide I want to spill so deeply into the city that no one can track me down. I need distance, and start down the Alhambra hill.

The walk doesn't disappoint. Last night's shadows have dripped down from the branches and now dance upon the gravel. I think again of Lorca, of the inspiration he drew from this hillside.

Heading left into Plaza Nueva, I enter the heart of town and walk for an hour, then dart into a tiny café for a shot of water and directions to the nearest hostel. One block up and two blocks over. Next to the Carnicería.

Paying my bill in advance, I go upstairs to my room. Of the four beds, only one is taken. A haphazard stack of postcards rests upon it.

The door to the bathroom swings open, and out he steps. Left lens fissured, hair matted wildly onto his head, same roly-poly gut hanging over the fold of his towel. The towel then comes untucked, falling painfully to the floor.

"Ah, roommates again." He comes towards me with his arms outstretched. "I am the big lucky, no?"

VALERIE PEHRSON IS A WRITER
LURKING IN THE ROCKY MOUNTAINS
OF COLORADO. SHE IS CURRENTLY A
STUDENT AT NAROPA UNIVERSITY AND
PLANNING A SEMESTER IN PRAGUE IN
THE SPRING OF 2004.

THE OTHER MENU

VALERIE PEHRSON

You can see where this is going already.

It was our first time in Europe, and our first time in Amsterdam, and we were staying in the heart of the Museumplein, just across from the Rijksmuseum and the Van Gogh Museum. My traveling companion and I had been in Paris for two weeks and, along with the rest of the nation, had celebrated with too much enthusiasm the release of the Beaujolais Nouveau. When we got off the train at Centraal Station, we had no idea what we were in for. Heineken beer by the barrelful? Yes. Coffee shops? Not right away, as we wanted to orient ourselves before diving into that particular curiosity. Displaying amazing self-control, we waited one entire day.

I am no longer a user of *Cannabis sativa*, and haven't been for many moons. Makes me funny in the head, you see, and not in a good way. But I used to enjoy it quite a bit. My friend, Tony, was an enthusiastic devotee of this little plant and after a bit of questioning of the locals, we were recommended a nice little neighborhood coffee shop. The Dutch we asked felt very strongly that our first experience should not be The Bulldog. It's the Hard Rock Cafe of coffee shops. So we jotted down directions and were on our way to the real deal.

We wandered down the *straat* a ways, ogling the shops and admiring the beautiful buildings, the canals, and the

AMSTERDAM

people packed on the busy thoroughfares. And the bicycles! Everywhere! You could get struck down if you didn't get out of the way after hearing the warning bell.

We found our destination after a bit of searching, as there was no discernable street address or sign to distinguish it from a private residence, and turned the shiny brass knob on the dark green door.

The light was subdued and it took a minute for our eyes to adjust to the dim, smoky atmosphere. At the far end of the room was the *barista*'s counter, where a platinum blonde was busy making coffees. On either side of the narrow room were plush couches and tables with candles burning. The clientele huddled together intimately in quiet conversation. The smell was unique, like sandalwood incense, oily coffee brewing, and something else, a sweet and sticky scent. We walked up to the counter.

"Would you like something to drink? Or would you like to see the smoke menu?"

"The other menu, first," said Tony. The woman nodded, and her co-worker emerged from a dark corner, gesturing for us to follow.

He was huge. Six foot who knows, and big, bald, and built like Mr. Clean. Tattoos covered both his arms. He led us down a claustrophobic staircase to a tiny antechamber under the stairs. *Open for Business*.

"This is your first time?" he asked. We nodded.

"Then I will be gentle." He giggled at his own joke, a sound that seemed out of place coming from such a huge frame, then pushed a small chalkboard across to us.

"Here is our menu and our prices. You will find them very reasonable and everything is of the finest quality."

I looked into the space behind him. It was unreal: an apothecary's chest of a room. As Tony browsed the menu, I couldn't get over the feeling that we were doing something illegal, so I made small talk, and asked Mr. Clean the Pusher about his tattoos.

"Some of them are fifteen years old. Not a lot of sun to damage them. Do you have any?"

I did, actually. Several.

"May I see them?"

Bundled up in so many layers of clothes, I didn't know if I could get to them, but my lower back was fairly accessible.

"That is very nice. Very nice place for ladies to have tattoo."

Tony finally made his selection, three grams of what was called Himalayan Gold. Mr. Clean weighed it out on a little scale for us, and when it came to the price, he said, "I will give you a deal because I like her tattoo." We were charged just four guilders for the little bag, and headed upstairs for our coffee treats.

At the counter, Tony ordered a frothy cappuccino and I asked for a pot of Assam tea. We looked around for a place to sit and chose a nook by the front window. I sat in the window seat and Tony planted himself on what looked to be a fortified ottoman. There was a low, small table in front of us, just big enough for our drinks, a candle, and the juice glass that was holding the rolling papers. Tony went to work preparing the joint while I stirred my tea and gazed out the window at the foot traffic coming off Damrak. It was misty and soft outside, the kind of weather I love. I couldn't get over the fact that my friend was sitting just two feet away from me rolling a huge joint, and we didn't have to worry about a thing.

"It will be fine, you'll see," Tony said as he licked the paper. Bending over the yellow candle, he lit the joint and took a long pull. As the smell hit my face, I suddenly flashed back to scenes of bathrooms in dance clubs, concerts, and the house I lived in with an old boyfriend.

"Vallie, honey, it's your hit," Tony said, the smoke creeping out around his teeth as he spoke.

Like riding a bike, there are some things you never forget. Pinching the joint between my fingers, I took a pull. It had a nice piney flavor and was rich without being sickly sweet. I held it in, feeling the effects right away.

Mr. Clean bounced over to our nook and unceremoniously plopped himself down beside me.

"So! This is your first time in Amsterdam? You are English?" he asked. "Americans?"

"We're Americans," I said, passing the joint back to Tony, over whose face spread a look like Christmas Eve.

"What do you think about my city? She is beautiful, yes? I have lived here my whole life." He was as proud as a new father.

"It's so overwhelming. It's a very *evolved* society, isn't it? Kids going home from school teasing each other in three or four languages? It amazes me. Between the coffee shops and the prostitutes, I don't understand how any work gets done in this country," I said.

"We are very proud to let people do as they wish." Then he changed the subject back to tattoos, and there and then, in front of the window, peeled off his white T-shirt to display a well-assembled collection of pectoral and abdominal muscles peppered with art. The pot had begun to kick in, and I was getting a little uneasy about the sailor-style bluebirds over each nipple, but I took another couple of hits. I mean, we'd come all this way. Might as well give it a go.

I offered Mr. Clean a hit. "I don't smoke," he said.

"Neither do I," I said, exhaling through my teeth.

Thankfully, just then the blonde behind the counter rang a little bell, and he had to attend to another client. Covering up his rippling, tattooed torso, he jogged across the hardwood floor to greet his new customers.

I looked at Tony, whose eyeballs were like two cherry tomatoes. He was grinning absurdly.

"Vallie's got a boyfriend," he sang.

"Let's get out of here and start wandering," I suggested. I didn't want to have to face that chest again, not in my vulnerable condition. We packed up our daypacks and re-bundled.

In the chilly November air, I smelled water for a moment before the cold robbed me of that particular sense. The light was almost painful after the darkness of the hash bar, and my brain was going a thousand miles a minute. I had been living on little more than oranges, espresso and wine for over two weeks, and my eyelids felt ridiculously heavy.

"Of course, all these suave sons-of-mothers know I'm ripped to the tits," I thought. I could smell the grime on myself, and wanted to hide in a hot shower and go to bed. Then we took a wrong turn. Instead of going left, which would have taken us back to Centraal Station, we went right and crossed the canal.

As we walked along, the streets got narrower, and began looking very much alike. It was like having that dream where the corridor keeps getting longer and longer, and you turn a corner to discover that you are in the same spot all over again. We did this for about an hour. There were no more canals, and it was as though the walls of the thin buildings were bending over.

I don't know when I realized that I was the only woman on the street. All I saw were variations of the color gray, and men. Lots of men, and they were looking at me strangely. Did they know how stoned I was? That's when it hit me. We were lost in the Red Light District. I'm not talking about the touristy part – there were no novelty peepshows, or History of Sex museums. This was IT. I was the only woman on the street because all the women here were *working*. I glanced up. Yes, about a foot and a half above my head there was one wearing little more than a dog collar and tall boots.

It sunk in that I was five thousand miles away from home and stoned out of my mind with a five-foot, three-inch-tall homosexual man. If we were to get rolled, I was going to have to take off my shoe and slap someone with its soggy weight to defend us.

I thought about the other places I had gotten lost. But this was foreign soil. These streets were packed with men doing what men do with women who get paid to do it. I became acutely aware of the clothes I was wearing, the way they touched my skin, my gait as I walked, my breasts under my thin blue leather coat. Men kept walking towards us, furtive weasel-glances on their sallow faces, frenzied hands in their pockets.

We turned a corner onto another narrow street, and another, and another. The boarded-up shop fronts were gray, the sky was gray, and everything smelled of urine, strong tobacco, and illicit sex. Finally, we turned one more corner, and above us, a bright green neon sign flashed:

*** GIRLS ***
*** DANCING ***
*** MAGAZINES ***

It was the most beautiful porn shop in the world. I had never been so happy to see a table full of dildoes and butt-plugs.

"You folks comin' for de peepshow? Pretty lady comin' to see de scenery? Dere is somethin' in here for everybody," said the Rastafarian man at the door. He had a kind face and generous, toothy smile that lit up like a beacon from heaven.

And he gave us directions out of there.

KAREN LEE BOREN ENDED UP STAYING
IN LONDON FOR TWO YEARS. SHE IS
CURRENTLY AN ASSISTANT PROFESSOR
AT RHODE ISLAND COLLEGE, AND
IS COMPLETING HER FIRST NOVEL.

THE QUEST

KAREN LEE BOREN

From the outside, the London Quest Hotel did not seem fantastic, or even particularly interesting. It crouched amiably amidst the seediness of Earl's Court, an area of London known as "Down Under" because of the abundance of Aussie and Kiwi youths who lived there while working to earn money to "do" Europe. The Kiwi woman who sat next to me on the train from Dover to Victoria Station told me in her clipped accent that the Quest was cheap, clean ("if you're not one of them picky Americans"), and would do until I could find some work. I scoffed with her at my per-snickety compatriots, certain that after a month in France of sleeping on night trains and showering in railway stations, if at all, I had sloughed off any inherited hygienic preoccupations. More importantly, I knew that after yet another plummet of the dollar and no work permit in hand, I didn't have the luxury of being fastidious.

I had an address and vague directions, but like most places in London, the Quest was still difficult to find. As I walked the length of Earl's Court Road, I played the London match game, trying to find street signs that corresponded with the wild maps in my *London A to Z*. Both my pack and my spirits were heavy and more than a little damp from the cold, steady mist, so when I turned onto Pembroke Road and saw the green-and-white sign grandly declaring *The London Quest*

LONDON

17

Hotel, I made the rash decision to stay there no matter how decrepit it turned out to be.

The price for a bed was six pounds per night, so an Australian woman with a ruddy face told me. As though refusing to believe that November could be anything but spring, she wore a tight Lycra tank top exposing the massive flesh of her arms, shoulders and upper back. Her buoyant breasts looked as though they might happily nourish triplets. Thrusting her fingers through the brass bars that made up the upper half of the reception door, she handed me a slip of paper on which the house rules were written. I looked at her bulky frame shoved into this tiny closet, and found myself feeling the same mixture of rage and sadness I felt at the zoo when I saw an animal housed in a pen too small for it to do anything but sit and stare gloomily at the crowds of people that filed past. But she didn't seem to mind her confinement, and when a spirited group of Swedes in the common room next to her tiny cage began demonstrating skiing techniques by shooshing off chairs and into each other, her voice boomed over theirs: "Keep your bloody feet off the furniture!"

Snatching the coins from my palm, she said, "You want a key?"

"To the room?" I asked.

"Yep."

"Well, yeah," I said. I had assumed such a thing would go without saying.

"It's another pound fifty, luv."

It was then that I realized that calling the London Quest a hotel was fairly optimistic on the part of the owners, but I was not to be daunted. The price, after all, was right. So I dragged my pack across the grimy carpeting to my room on the first of six floors. It was jammed full with eight steel cots piled in twos like berths in a ship, its manila-yellow walls blank but for the numerous scuff marks from the cots' steel frames. A double lancet window with stained-glass panes had been cut into the far wall, giving the room an illusion of height. At the foot of each cot were a folded pumpkin-colored blanket, flat sheet, deflated pillow encased in stiff white cotton, and a list of shower room rules. I was later informed by Annie, the voluptuous manager, that the shower was available for only two hours each day. "So no lally-gaggin', eh?" she warned, the wattle of her tricep wagging with her finger.

The aisle between the cots was just wide enough to walk through, but various backpacks, their colorful contents spilling out, jutted from beneath the beds, obstructing even this small path. After tripping several times, I hoisted my own pack onto one of the top bunks, thankful that without a bureau or wardrobe, there was no need to unpack.

Thus relieved of my burden, I began to investigate the putrid but oddly familiar odor that hung in the small room, aware that I may not have shed my antiseptic Americanism as thoroughly as I had imagined. Though I was reputed to have the strongest sniffer in my family of eight, I couldn't identify the stench. It was certainly something familiar, but it had none of the pleasant tones associated with horse manure or rotting fruit. Rather, it was chemical, and reminded me of the tanning factory near my home in Milwaukee, but there was something more human about this smell, something sinister. No matter its origin, the stink was pervasive. As pungent right in front of the window's small slats as away, it did not seem to emanate from any particular source.

This fetid scent would plague me throughout the duration of my stay at the Quest. It infiltrated my dreams to the point where I spent my unconscious hours wandering through dirty locker rooms, dripping sewers and skunk-infested woods. After a time, I became certain it had permeated all of my clothing, my hair and even my skin. I blamed it for the lethargy into which I would fall for the three months of my stay. For now, though, I didn't worry; I merely angled the window slats to allow more air flow, and went out for coffee.

The Quest served only breakfast – a hard roll, jam and coffee – but I found there was a small kitchen where guests could cook other meals, and a tiny refrigerator for storing food, although it was doubtful that anything left one day would be there the next. The dining room had a television and VCR on which there was always playing one of the five movies Annie checked out to the guests.

Tonight, and every night for the next week, *Dog Day Afternoon* ran four times in a row. Lodgers watched with varying degrees of interest, directly proportional to the length of their stay thus far. Occasionally, those who had been forced to endure the film for months on end would chant along with Pacino: "AT-TI-CA! AT-TI-CA!" Sometimes two or three people would take parts and act out the scenes to perfection. Those less interested smoked cigarettes while talking of home and playing backgammon, reading old magazines or planning their next trips.

It seemed that the kids from "Down Under" were expected to travel the way American kids were expected to go to college: the longer they stayed away, the more prestige they gained with their mates back home. Because the airfare was so expensive from Australia and New Zealand, and because as members of the Commonwealth they could work legally, London became a rest and work stop between journeys. They worked hard at lousy jobs – waitressing, nannying, construction or on factory lines – and they drank even harder. They also fucked often and indiscreetly, as I was to quickly discover.

Exhausted from my journey, I retired to my bunk after the second run of *Dog Day*. The stench hit me violently as I opened the door to my room. It smelled of decaying bodies, flatulence, sweat socks and things my olfactory glands could not even place. After a final whiff of fresh air, I flashed the lights on – then off again when I saw that people were already asleep in the beds. Under the light of a streetlamp, tinged blue by the stained glass, I pulled off my jeans and T-shirt, too tired to care that some of my sleeping roommates were male. Annie hadn't mentioned anything about the rooms being co-ed, but by this point it seemed only a minor detail. Pulling on a clean shirt, I made my bed in a rudimentary fashion while trying not to step on the knees and elbows of the unconscious man in the bunk below mine. With my hands shielding my nostrils, I fell quickly asleep.

If I had been brought up in California, I would have thought it was an earthquake that jarred me awake. Milwaukee had only the duel-pistoned Ladish Hammer which forged steel and shook the ground throughout the night. When I was awakened by the jiggling of my bed, I assumed the third-shift factory workers had thrown the hammer's switch. One sniff of the rancid air brought the reality of my location back to me, and the moans issuing from beneath my bunk made the source of the quakes all too clear.

The absurdity of other people's sex is impossible to ignore when one is perched above them in the dark, unwillingly along for the ride. At first I was embarrassed, as though I had walked in on someone in the bathroom. I tried not to move. The rhythm quickened, the breaths became breathier, and skin slapped against skin. I couldn't help picturing cartoon fish flopping on dry land, and stifled an adolescent giggle, remembering childhood laughing fits during Mass. Attempting to resist my urge to laugh, I tried to imagine who was "down under." Surely it wasn't the scared-looking blonde who had seemed so scandalized by Pacino's would-be transsexual lover. Perhaps it was the lusty woman who sucked sour balls as she played checkers? I couldn't stand the mystery any longer and leaned over the edge of my cot to peek. In the light of the street-lamp I saw it: like a medal of honor, "100% Grade A" was tattooed onto the skin of Annie's fleshy, flopping buttocks.

For the three months I shared the charms of the London Quest, I would drink more beer, smoke more hash, and sip more coffee than is healthy even for the young. I would learn of the malleability of time, which can stretch a minute into a mile's length, and compress a month into the space of a single bed. I would learn to sleep late and eat often, to snooze through the sounds of sex, and to tolerate the bodies of strangers. I would move from bad to worse, into a squat in the center of Camden Town. And though I would never know the source of the Quest's pungency, within its walls I would, like Tennyson's lotus-eaters, learn, live, and lie reclined.

section27
(8 replies)

Walk on by

Hello. I am going to London on Saturday and was wondering the best way to walk. Do I move quite slowly with my head down, do I hurry along jumping slightly every third or fourth step, or do I develop a theatrical limp? I just don't know!

mrsteve38
1.

Try . . .

using a pogo stick!

– Stephen Clay

eric boquist
2.

Check with . . .

the Ministry of Silly Walks

dancingbunny
3.

A common one . . .

is to walk very fast, no eye contact, pretend everything's getting in your way and that you're about to whack someone! Perfect. Although I think the others will go down well too.

MaestroMan
4.

If you want to act like a real tourist,

just amble about all over the place, getting in as many people's way as possible.

Oh, and don't forget to stand on the left on the escalators!

abscend
5.

to cover all bases . . .

. . . cycle all types of walk mentioned every 10–15 paces. and grin hugely at all times. Londoners don't particularly take to smiling from 0900–1700. the pogo walk is common, ye, so use that pogo stick!

FartherTed
6.

Tourists

In order to perfect your walking like a tourist be sure to stop at the top of escalators and look at your map!

I have this on good authority from my mate who works at the Department of Walking Up Stairs Two at a Time!

myrrinda
7.

don't forget

to walk like a tourist, you must make sure to wear a huge backpack, swing around wildly hitting everyone in sight, and stop abruptly every ten steps to try and figure out where you are, and if you're indeed going the right way.

GemmaPurves
8.

and attach a fluffy toy on a long string

so you get a whipping effect.

Walk in a zigzag.

Never apologize for bruising/maiming others – it's their fault!

THE EDITOR OF THIS ANTHOLOGY,
LISA JOHNSON JUGGLES A WRITING
CAREER WITH MOTHERHOOD. SHE
WONDERS HOW LONG HER THREE-YEAR-
OLD SON IZZY COULD LAST ON THE
PLANE RIDE TO EUROPE.

THE PROFESSIONAL
LISA JOHNSON

Row after row of pale green buildings stretched down the street. Old women draped themselves over their railings, the ashes from their cigarettes drifting down toward the concrete. Though communism had gradually loosened its hold on Eastern Europe, an atmosphere of despair still lingered.

After two weeks on the trains of Italy and Greece, I was ready to drop. Dumping my daypack on the steps of the school dormitory, I pressed the bell. Thank God it was only 7 p.m. I'd been told someone would be around until nine every night.

Here in Szekszard, a tiny village famous only for its wine festivals, it was apparent that most people had never seen an American before. Socialism had been out for a number of years, but the Hungarians still struggled to replace the Russian language with something more international.

Thus, my new job. I was to spend a full year teaching high-school students English. After weeks of preparation, I'd decided to bring along photos of the Empire State Building, an abundance of Levi's, and a bunch of Bugs Bunny comics, and had dropped off the bulk of my belongings two weeks before. I'd brought along live entertainment as well – my boyfriend, a heavy metal rock guitarist turned schoolteacher for the occasion. Imagining the rapt faces of future students, our plans for them included cultivating Chia

HUNGARY

24

herb pets and creating bumper stickers with their own personal mantras.

There was no answer on the first ring, so I pressed the bell again and waited. The sky changed to indigo, and suddenly something stirred a few yards away. In a green dumpster at the end of the property, two people were digging. With a large thin stick, an old man removed chunks of bread from the trash bin, stuffing them into a white plastic bag held by an even older woman.

Gypsies. I had been warned about them, for in Hungary these dark-skinned immigrants remained on the lowest rung of society, scorned for their color and way of life.

We were the lucky ones, I thought, imagining the fish soup and homemade noodles that surely awaited us on the other side of the door.

"What's taking so long?" Tony called up from the bottom of the stairs. Snapping my eyes back to the door, I held the bell down for ten more seconds. Its loud ringing was cut short, as if someone had suddenly turned off the sound, yet nobody came.

"What the hell's her problem?" Tony asked, watching a figure on the top balcony across the street begin to gesture furiously, then slam her door.

"Who knows?" The bell was now silent, no matter how long or hard I pushed.

Fifteen more minutes went by. I had no cash whatsoever, had counted on being taken care of once we arrived.

Then something bony poked me in the shoulder. Whirling around, I met the knit gray eyebrows of the gesticulating woman from across the street. She wagged her finger, releasing a cloud of stale breath into my face.

"*Nincsen!*" She grabbed my arm. I tried to extract myself, but she held on.

"No speak Hungarian," I stammered. Loosening her hold to point to her watch, she yelled something even more unintelligible.

"*Nem tudom.*" The one Hungarian phrase I had committed to memory suddenly appeared in my mouth: I don't know. "*Nem tudom* Hungarian."

"*Hat!*" Livid, she pointed to the six on the watch face.

"What the hell?" Tony said. "Can't they tell time in this country?"

"*Holnap! Hat!*" she insisted, shaking her head vehemently.

"You think she means six o'clock tomorrow?"

"Oh, man," he muttered. "These goddamn people."

"Stop it," I told him. "I bet she'll offer us a place to stay. Let me just try to tell her who we are."

Turning back to face her, I plastered a smile on my face. "*Tanar!*" I proclaimed, banging a finger against my chest. "English *tanar*! English teacher!"

"*Holnap!*" Shaking her head no, she threw up her hands and trotted back to her block of flats, vanishing into its dark front doors.

"What the fuck are we gonna do?" Tony pulled a pack of Marlboros from his pocket and stomped down the street.

It was now completely dark except for the lights of apartment windows and a few streetlamps. I planted myself on the steps, then got up again to lug our two heavy backpacks together as a makeshift bed. Tony returned a little while later, and we pressed between them, but the chill made its way through our body heat.

What a welcome.

Around one in the morning, I forced myself slowly toward the dumpster. Squatting near its darkest corner, I waited for jeering faces, the sudden jab of cold metal.

At 5:27, the first streaks of light began appearing. Pushing the doorbell again, I could make out its faint echo inside.

"Someone's playing games with us." Tony rubbed his eyes and lit another cigarette. Through the glass something moved, and a sleepy woman with red hair sprayed into a mini beehive marched to the door.

So this was the gatekeeper.

"*Tanar*," I mouthed, tapping the glass. She thrust the door open, staring at my bloodshot eyes and matted hair. "English *tanar*."

Blinking twice, she motioned me inside, turning her face from the scent of my body, and pushed open another door which led to a tiny office. On one wall was a wooden board with hooks and keys. Beneath it, a cardboard calendar, with a prominent painting of the Statue of Victory, displayed the days in Hungarian. Glancing at me suspiciously, she jabbed her finger at one of the dates. *August 30*. I squinted at my name printed beneath. She folded her arms across her chest and looked at me without expression.

It was August 27.

"English *tanar*," I repeated. So what if I was three days early? "Those are mine." I gestured to the set of keys I'd been given two weeks before.

She paused, sighing heavily. After closely examining the calendar once more, she finally removed my keyring from the peg and exited briskly.

I followed her down the hallway to the last room on the right. Pushing the key into the lock, she opened the door at last.

I was "home." The things I'd dropped off previously lined the wooden shelves: two necklaces of love beads, a picture of my sisters and me in New York, the pair of sunglasses I thought I'd lost.

"It's me!" I grabbed the photo and shoved it toward her. "See?" She reluctantly removed it from my hand, frowning.

"*Tanar*," I confirmed. The matter was settled.

Then she smiled. Putting her hand on my back, she encouraged me toward the door.

"Maybe it's a surprise," I thought. "The real welcome's coming." I allowed her to usher me back out, and scanned the dim hallway for smiling faces, listening for the pop of wine bottles.

All was quiet. Empty. Beaming vacantly, she placed the key back in the door, and with an efficient click, locked me out.

FREELANCE WRITER GAIL COCHRANE
BELIEVES THE TRAVELS SHE HAS
TAKEN HAVE GIVEN HER THE
PERSPECTIVE AND COURAGE TO UNDER-
TAKE MORE PERSONAL JOURNEYS:
THOSE STRENUOUS EXCURSIONS TO
SELF-KNOWLEDGE.

NIGHT PASSAGE

GAIL COCHRANE

I came onto the ferry amongst an excited commotion of French and British foot passengers rushing to secure a spot and line up for the cafeteria. As the reclining seats were filling quickly, I dropped my backpack on an empty one in the front row and noticed a girl sitting alone a few seats away. Hoping she spoke English, I figured we could pass the time together.

The French ferry would cross the English Channel in the black of night, arriving in Le Havre at 6 a.m. Taking off my heavy wool sweater and one of the lighter ones I wore underneath, I arranged my stuff for the night then went to buy a yogurt for dinner.

The lights were dimmed while people continued to rustle around. Like a murder of crows they settled briefly, then rose up to rustle around more before roosting again. I watched the girl, envying her ease. Casually dressed in jeans and stylish boots, she had a striking face, wide-set gray eyes, and thick hair bundled into a knot at the back of her head. She appeared so free: she had no luggage or handbag, not even a paper bag with food for the night.

My hopes for conversation died, however, when she caught me watching her. Frowning, she crossed her long legs and faced the other way.

One of the deck hands then approached, his back ramrod straight, and stopped in front of the girl. After sweeping his

THE ENGLISH CHANNEL

28

eyes up and down her body, he jerked his head towards a door, turned on his heel and strode away. The girl threw me a quick glance before rising to follow.

The engines rumbled steadily, vibrating up through my tennis shoes until I pushed back the recliner and unrolled the heavy wool ferry blanket, pulling it to my chin. The lights dimmed completely, leaving me with nothing to do but pursue sleep. I dozed uneasily as the ferry began to pitch sharply to one side and roll slowly back to the other. This happened again and again. There was a rustle of paper bags and the unmistakable sound of retching. Saliva flooded my mouth and, having no idea where the bags were to be found, I turned my mind resolutely away from the growing chorus. The exciting accommodations of an hour ago were now dark and cold, and smelled of vomit. Filled with a longing for home, I tried to focus on overcoming my own seasickness, but found I couldn't shake a nagging worry about where the girl had been taken.

The hours passed, and at first light I gladly left my chair to go to the rest rooms. While splashing a thin stream of tepid water on my face, the door opened and shut behind me. It was the girl from the night before. Her hair had come out of its neat bun and fell about her face in wild disarray. A potent, musky scent – like the underside of a decaying log, rank and gamy – wafted from her. Studiously I put the paste on my toothbrush and watched her reflection in the mirror. She ran her fingers fruitlessly through the tangled hair and leaned close to the mirror, fingering her swollen red lips. Then the gray eyes shot over to catch me staring – they were clear and sharp and full of contempt.

Embarrassed, I looked back at my own reflection: my red-rimmed eyes and limp hair. Gathering my things and holding my breath, I got ready to leave. But at the door I paused, glancing back. She stood with her hands on her hips watching me go, her ruby lips curled in a small, scornful smile.

At 6 a.m. the haggard passengers streamed down the ramp past the captain and his officers. The men were in high spirits, looking sharp in their navy uniforms. They had obviously fared the passage much better than their charges. I couldn't help but wonder how many of them had had her. Even their gold buttons winked in the early morning sun.

DAVE FOX LEADS TOURS IN
SCANDINAVIA AND WRITES FOR A
VARIETY OF TRAVEL PUBLICATIONS.
MORE OF HIS TRAVEL AND COMIC
WRITING CAN BE FOUND AT WWW.DAVE
THEFOX.COM.

FINNISH SAUNAS:
THE NAKED TRUTH

DAVE FOX

I was sweating profusely in the 88-degree heat. That's 88 degrees
Celsius – 190 Fahrenheit. But it wasn't the sauna that was making
me uncomfortable – it was the fact that I was sitting there alone,
screamingly naked in a public place, and not sure if I was supposed
to be nude or clothed.

It had been a dreary, drizzly day in Helsinki. Rather than eating
waffles in the rain at the outdoor market, I'd gone back early to the
ship that would take me to Stockholm overnight. For about forty
euros, I could have a one-hour massage and ninety minutes in the
ship's spa.

A lot of people have the wrong idea about so-called "Swedish
massages." They don't feel good while you're having one, and they're
too intense to be done by petite Scandinavian cuties named Inga. But
they are effective in beating your tension into submission.

For fifty-five minutes, a burly Finnish man induced more
pain on my back than I knew was possible using only two
thumbs. The first time I screamed, he muttered about tight
muscles. The second time, he offered to lighten up, which he
did for all of thirty seconds. But I breathed into the pain, let
my muscles buckle, and walked out feeling blissfully mellow,
albeit bruised.

There were four other activities: soaking in the whirlpool,
sitting in the steam room, taking a sauna, or drinking beer.

FINLAND

30

Never mind that beer is not usually recommended while participating in dehydrating activities such as these. This was Finland, and drinking alcohol is how Finns replace their fluids.

The whirlpool had room for about ten people – potential strangers sitting close together – so swimsuits made sense. The steam room right next to the whirlpool also looked like a keep-yourself-covered kind of place. I asked the attendant to be sure, but it was when I was handed a key to the locker room and sauna that confusion began.

I'm not one of those prudish Americans who are terrified of being seen nude in public, just as long as everyone else is nude as well. And my other sauna experiences have always been uncovered. Scandinavians don't have the hang-ups about nudity that Americans do. On warm, sunny days, I'd seen people strip completely naked in city parks.

In public saunas, I'd encountered separate rooms for men and women, but here there was no sign on the door to indicate if the sexes were separated. I was the only person in the room so far, and so I sat, dreading the possibility of an innocent Finnish granny entering upon my inappropriate state of undress.

The only scenario worse than this was being clothed in a place where one was supposed to be naked. I imagined the comments on the boat later that evening: "Hey Toivo, there goes the American with the swimsuit in the sauna! I wonder what he has to hide?"

I couldn't ask the attendant again; she'd think I was obsessed. So I decided to keep my swimsuit on.

The purpose of a sauna is to sweat every drop of water out of your body, and then shock it with a quick, cold shower. The room's interior is all wood, with a heater with rocks on top of it in one corner. Scooping water out of a nearby bucket onto the rocks creates a wall of steam that hits you like dragon's breath.

After ten minutes of this, I decided my bathing suit was ridiculous. I showered and went in for round two with only a towel.

But it was still too warm. No, this had to be the place to be naked. Dropping the towel from my waist, I sat. I sweated. I worried. I couldn't stop thinking about the granny.

Finally, I decided to leave. This was too stressful.

From the whirlpool, I watched the locker room door but no one went in. So I headed for the Turkish bath, a delightful, steamy, herb-scented dream. I relaxed, until I looked up at the ceiling and spotted the dodgy-looking steam valves.

I wanted to go back into the sauna, but was determined not to return until I knew the rules. This left only one last activity: beer.

Sitting at the bar, I sipped slowly, never taking my eyes off the locker room door. Finally, just as I was about to give up, a married couple walked in. They paid at the counter, rented swimsuits, and were sent to separate saunas. At last I could be certain that naked strangers of the opposite sex would not be in close quarters! I had it all figured out now.

Swigging one last gulp of beer, I strolled confidently into the locker room. It was the only time in my life I was happy to see a hairy, flabby, naked man. He nodded. I nodded. He headed for the shower. Undressing, I headed for the sauna.

Opening the door a crack, I peeked inside, then slammed it shut, horrified. The two men inside were wearing bathing suits!

I didn't get it. What was with the separate rooms, then? And why was Hairy Flabby Naked Man showering right outside without anything on? I went back and resuited.

Entering the sauna again, one of the men inside moved over to make room. I thanked him in Norwegian. He answered in Swedish, but his accent was from somewhere else. He was as foreign as I was!

I sighed. Hairy Flabby Naked Man was about to walk, fully exposed, into a room full of foreigners. I wondered if *he'd* feel intimidated.

When he finally entered wearing a black swimsuit, I gave up. All I knew for sure was that he looked far more offensive in a skimpy black Speedo than he did *au naturelle*.

One by one, my sauna mates left until I was alone again. My ninety minutes were just about up. Undressing one last time, I showered in blissful, naked privacy.

BORN, RAISED AND CURRENTLY
RESIDING IN RHODE ISLAND, JOHN
MORGAN BECAME HOOKED ON TRAVEL
AFTER STUDYING ABROAD AT THE
UNIVERSITY OF SYDNEY. A RECENT
GRADUATE AND CURRENT ENTREPRENEUR,
HIS PASSIONS ARE MUSIC, READING,
WRITING, FITNESS, OUTDOORS,
PHOTOGRAPHY, CULTURE, HISTORY,
MATH, PHYSICS AND PHILOSOPHY.

WAKING UP TO WINTER:
JOHN MORGAN

A Thorn Tree Post

I'm breathing with a light and free feeling as I disembark my plane.
It's a feeling of release and independence as I begin my European
journey. Backpacking somehow sets me apart from everyone. Even
in this airport. True, people here are traveling, but they each have
things to do, deadlines to meet, particular people to visit, itineraries
to follow, specific things to see. Not me, I'm different. I have
everywhere to go and anything to see. My destination is culture and
knowledge and experience. Although I'm traveling amongst scores
of others, I am different.

It's my first time in Italy and I just need my bag, then I can
float around aimlessly. What's a backpacker worth without their
backpack?

Upon leaving the baggage claim, I attempt to follow the signs to
the trains. I find a machine and buy a ticket. All I can understand
is the track number and time. Good enough.

Almost as soon as I climb aboard, I know something is wrong by
the way the train conductor is talking to some other
Americans. Something is the matter with their tickets. Well
I'm sure my ticket is correct at least. Nope. *Parla inglese?*
"Validate!" *Oh . . . sorry, I didn't know I needed to validate
my ticket.* "When you come to Italia, you speak Italia!"

Oh geeze . . .

ROME

33

I'm frustrated with this man for giving me trouble because I don't speak fluent Italian. I'm coming to visit his country because it's a wonderful place! He should be grateful! Err . . . well, actually I don't really agree with this initial defensive attitude. I remember I'm in a place foreign to me, not foreign to him. If I want to make this place unforeign to me, then that is my responsibility. So, within a minute, I go from being frustrated to realizing I'm wrong to actually reflect on what just happened. I'm even smiling and chuckling a bit to myself.

When you come to Italia, you speak Italia! This, only an hour after my arrival in Rome, is a sharp reminder that when in Rome, do as the Romans do.

The train pulls into the station and I move for the exit before we come to a halt. I head for the door at a timid rate, which seems to solicit quite a few comments from those in more of a hurry than me. I don't want to stand out too much, so I step up the pace and walk briskly but aimlessly. I don't think anyone notices that I don't know where I'm going.

I have a hostel in mind, so I figure I should call and find out how to get there. Of course, a sweet voice with an Australian accent answers. I wonder if Australians run over half the hostels in the world. It seems that way. Anyway, I get directions to Hostel Alesandro and head out into the street.

My first taste of the brisk Roman air is quite a mouthful. Every city has a scent to it, but this is intense. I can taste the noisy mopeds almost as much as I can hear them. A whiff from a nearby bakery overpowers the smell of grease and oil, and demands a deep breath. Maybe fifteen strides pass and I have already become accustomed to this new air.

I eventually reach the hostel, which is a nice place. I check in and then toss my pack into the pile of packs owned by other trusting travelers. I can't help but wonder if anyone will touch my stuff. I'm so accustomed to worrying about my possessions, day in and day out, that it's hard not to think about my belongings sitting in an accessible pile, alone for hours. Everyone else is doing it though, so I suppose I need not be concerned. We're all independent travelers and there's that mutual respect and trust. Somehow that's never enough to make me completely comfortable though. Just to be safe, I secure the essentials inside my daypack.

It's a fun feeling, knowing I'm carrying everything I need to survive in one small bag. I head back out into the streets with a lighter load. The sun is setting and my stomach is growling. I decide to see as much as I can before dark, then grab something to eat. I am awestruck by the sights, so unlike home. This city was built well before beauty began to be sacrificed for efficiency.

I'm taking everything in: all of it. The colors, sizes and shapes of the buildings and monuments, the chainsaw-like sounds of the mopeds, the high-pitched European car horns, the smell of the out-door markets and leather shops. I think about how truly immense our world is. It boggles my mind that so many millions of people in so many millions of places all over the world have their own lives, their own circle of friends, their own homes. This place, so foreign to me, is home to so many people. I begin to think about how everything that makes one place or people foreign to another, is the result of our own creations: language, culture, government, religion. At the very heart, we are all humans and we all basically live life the same way. We always have and we always will. The only force that separates us and, ironically, brings us together, is our minds.

As I walk the streets of Rome this evening, I feel like I'm fighting a battle against human separation. By trying to see and learn I am making one more place in this world less foreign to me, and myself less foreign to the world.

At this thought, a sudden rush of excitement about the weeks to come sends chills down my spine.

Back at the hostel, I prepare for my first hang-out-and-meet-people-in-the-common-area session of this trip. I've got my guidebook handy, so I can look occupied as I scope out the situation. The tele-vision is on and they're talking about news in America. I'm quickly reminded just how much my country is forced into the faces of everyone on our planet. It's like our culture – or multi-culture or anti-culture or whatever we have – is smothering the rest of the world. I'm wondering how many non-Americans in the room are thinking about the same thing and hate my country right now. I think I'll wait until after the news to speak up.

Oh! Hi Britney Spears! I should have guessed "MTV Italia" would come on next. I give up waiting for America to stop jumping around like an idiot on the television, and strike up a conversation with the loud Dutch guy at the table. *How long have you been here? Where did you come from? Where are you going?* Etc. The questions are routine, but everyone is always genuinely interested in the responses. They're also guaranteed to spark conversation in the room. Someone has always been there last week or is going there tomorrow. Talk about travel, with a roomful of like-minded people, is motivating and exciting. Hearing all the descriptions and stories, in all the different languages and accents, about all the places people have gone quickly passes time and ignites friendships.

Finally, I say my mellow goodnights and scuff my feet up the stairs and into my room. The beds, which held only bags before, are now filled with motionless bodies. It's time I get some much-needed rest.

- 2:12 a.m. I'm woken by the loud Dutch guy storming back into the hostel after hitting the pubs. "WHO VANTS TO PAHTEEEEEEE?" I put my headphones back on and start the CD over.
- 3:40 a.m. I'm woken by snoring. At first I'm amused by the differing frequencies of the two snorers, causing the snores to go in and out in time with each other, but I quickly become annoyed. I jam the headphones deeper into my ears and replay the CD.
- 5:20 a.m. Awoken by a fellow traveler who has decided to wait until morning to pack. Why is it that people who pack in the morning always seem to have noisy paper or plastic bags to mess around with? Every zipper zipped and every clip clipped is loud and painful. His meek attempt to dull the pain by moving ever so slowly does nothing but prolong the torture. I chuckle to

myself while driving my headphones deeper into my cranium. I know I'm guilty of making the same early morning racket from time to time.

- 6:36 a.m. The sun blasts through the shutters on the hostel window. It becomes obvious that my bunk was the last choice for a reason. Even with my eyes closed, the early morning sun blinds me. It's not worth fighting it anymore. I'll catch up on sleep tomorrow. I hop down with surprising energy, my bare feet slapping the cold hostel floor. I slide on sandals and grab my toiletries and travel towel.

The one bonus of rising early is clean showers. It takes me a few minutes to work the strange lock on the shower door and to balance my clothes, towel and gear on the seat-level shelf in the shower. I wonder if anyone ever actually sits on this thing. Who sits down in the shower? Once I complete the balancing act, I turn to my next assignment. I'm facing three knobs with no labels. I figure I have a one-third chance of getting scalded with hot water, a one-third chance of getting blasted with ice-cold water and a one-third chance of getting it right. I stand close to the wall, attempting to miss the spray. COLD COLD! I frantically turn the other knob . . . HOT HOT DAMN HOT! Turning the cold knob all the way does nothing; it can't overpower the practically boiling water. I'm quickly surrounded by a warm fog and nearly become disoriented, but I finally find that turning the hot knob nearly all the way off solves my problem.

I make my way through cleaning quickly, unsure of how long a hot shower will last here. I'm not surprised that my towel and clothes are wet: it's near impossible to find a dry spot in hostel showers. I dry myself with my damp towel and put on my wet clothes. I imagine that as I travel from town to town and stay in new places every couple of nights, small things like this will affect the smoothness of normal activities. As soon as I get a handle on the shower here, I'll move on and face the same challenge at another hostel. I don't think I could ever measure the number of factors that make a constant environment comfortable.

After a quick breakfast, I decide to visit Vatican City. I head to the subway and emerge a block's walk from the Vatican. As I saunter around the corner at the end of the block, I face a giant castle wall. The size and length of this wall is quite amazing, but what's even more astonishing is the number of people lined up along it – and it's not even 8 a.m. But after a surprisingly short wait, I reach the Vatican entrance. If, before today, I had to pick one place in the world where I didn't think there would be a McDonald's, I just might have picked Vatican City. To my embarrassment, the big yellow arches sit practically over the entrance.

I spend half the day finding my way through this monstrous maze of an art gallery. I walk down what seems like miles of hallways lined with sculptures. Each of these masterpieces really deserves its own place in which to display its magnificence, but the overwhelming number of them makes that impossible. There are mosaics everywhere. I'm walking on art that would be found behind glass and guard at home.

As I turn into each new room, I wonder if this is it: is this the Sistine Chapel? Yes, this is it! Oh . . . no it's not. I think it's the next one. This goes on for hours. Eventually, I find myself in a chapel with an obvious and overwhelming difference from the rest: the largest and most crowded of all the chapels is also the most calm and quiet. Michelangelo's Sistine Chapel necessitates no discussion between its visitors. Barely a sound echoes through this room. It is filled with faces from all the earth, aimed in all directions, attempting to take in all they can. I remember these images from photos and from books, and now I realize their pictorial representation does only minor justice. I am not seeing, I'm experiencing. I am not looking, I'm dreaming. I am not believing, I'm praying. I leave awestruck, reliving the experience in a surreal daydream.

It's well past midnight when I decide to get up at 4 a.m. for the three-hour train ride to Naples. I hardly get any shut-eye before a sprint to the train station in the pitch dark and freezing cold. Once on board, I assume a contorted position, but am tired enough to lose myself in another short sleep.

Beethoven's *Moonlight Sonata* is playing softly in my head-phones. Daylight begins to break and wakes me from my intermittent slumber. Leaning my head on the window has made me shivering cold and left the glass so fogged that only shapes and colors are visible. The vibrations of the train are rattling my jaw and I'm quite stiff from the position my body is kinked in. However, I choose not to move. Instead I lie still, listening to the piano dance, memorizing the scent of this train and watching a golden sun light up the Italian countryside. I find such solace in the present that not a single thought is necessary. I'm uncomfortable, I'm dirty, I'm tired and I'm cold, but somehow . . . waking up to winter has never felt better.

TOM SMITH TEACHES ENGLISH AT PENN
STATE IN ABINGTON, A SUBURB OF
PHILADELPHIA. HE WRITES ON AUTO-
BIOGRAPHY AND TWENTIETH-CENTURY
LITERATURE, AND HAS RECENTLY
TRAVELED TO AUSTRALIA.

TAKEN IN

TOM SMITH

Having grown up in the fishbowl of a small town of five thousand people and spending two years in a college known as a "pressure cooker," I wanted unfamiliar faces, fresh experiences, and a new self.

In Paris, after wandering through Sacré Coeur and looking out over the city from the parapet in front of the vast basilica, I wandered westward toward place Blanche, hoping to savor the Montmartre I had imagined – artists and models in studios, sidewalk cafes buzzing with conversation, dappled light filtering through the trees.

What I saw instead were grimy city streets, neglected shop fronts, steel bars covering dusty windows, and, eventually, a huge, pinkish red neon sign announcing the *Moulin Rouge*. I walked in. Momentarily blinded by the dark, I stumbled to a table in the middle of the room, sat down, and watched as a woman on stage lazily crooned a French song I'd never heard, accompanied by a minimal orchestra.

Within a minute or two, a waiter came by and I ordered a Kronenbourg. Soon after the beer arrived, so did a smiling, well-padded woman, overly made up by my prudish American standards. She pulled up a chair close to me, asked sweetly if I was American, and seemed especially pleased to find out that I was. After a few minutes of awkward conversation, my

FRANCE

40

French as bad as her English, she began to pout and asked why I hadn't offered to buy her a drink.

"Of course. What do you want?" Instantly, her manner changed. Suddenly all business, she signaled for the waiter, quickly relayed what I took to be her order, and asked me for ten dollars to cover it. After I gave her the cash, she excused herself, to go to the powder room, I assumed.

While I waited, my attention drifted to the melancholy singer, unhappy about something I would never understand. Lights a muted shade of the pinkish red of the neon sign outside bathed the small dusty stage, and the few scattered customers sat absorbed in their drinks or companions. Minutes passed. No sign of my new friend.

I patiently enjoyed the entertainment, the effect of the beer, and the freedom of being on my own in Paris – in the Moulin Rouge, no less, in the middle of a weekday afternoon.

As more time passed, pleasant thoughts slowly gave way to the uneasy realization that the friendly Frenchwoman was not going to come back, that I had been deftly separated from a ten-dollar bill, and that the waiter was the accomplice in this all-too-easy fleecing of an American hick.

I hoped the dark hid my embarrassment and shame. Not wanting to reveal the innocent dupe I was, I calmly finished my beer and walked out slowly, feigning obliviousness. On the subway back to my shabby little hotel room on the Left Bank near the Pantheon, where I savored Hemingway's *A Moveable Feast* when not writing in my journal, I chastised myself for having been taken in, and was determined never to be gulled so easily again.

Some time later, I hitchhiked to the South of France, taking mostly silent rides with people whose English was as minimal as my French. My destination was Avignon, and by the time I stood on the esplanade outside the Palais des Papes, looking up at its pale, creamy stone towers, it was late afternoon. A weak December sun sat low in an indifferently gray sky, and it was getting colder. As I headed east across the rushing Rhône toward the city's hostel, I saw the famous bridge on my right and hummed the children's song: "*Sur le pont d'Avignon, L'on y danse, l'on y danse.*" Like all of Avignon, it stood there as if it had always existed, as if it had risen out of the earth to form itself into shapes perfectly adapted for human use.

It was Christmas Eve, but Paris had eaten a hole in my budget, and I had to economize. In a small market I bought a baguette, a chunk of Swiss cheese, and a bottle of vile "orange squash," much cheaper than orange juice, but with some vitamins and nutritional value, I hoped.

The gray stone hostel was perched at the edge of the city on a hilly side street, surrounded by scrabbly naked trees. Inside, a dark-haired, thirtyish man in an old sweater and jeans emerged from the back of the building. I assumed he was a graduate student who earned extra money by running the hostel. He said that because it was Christmas Eve, no one else was staying over and there would be no meal. If I wanted to stay the night, however, I could.

I went to my assigned room on the second floor and ate a little bread and cheese, washing it down with the sugary, orange-flavored liquid. Around seven, I walked downstairs to the common area to write up the day's entry in my journal. Beneath a single exposed bulb dangling from the ceiling, I sat on a shabby sofa and spun my traveler's tale on a well-worn card table. Time vanished. When I looked up, it was well after eight. I needed to stretch and went outside.

Fierce stars in an ink-black sky blinked untranslatable messages. A biting north wind blew in my face, whipping trees and careening around corners. The swiftly moving Rhône broke up reflections of the white lights of Avignon as it sped on its way to the sea. On the opposite shore, the palace towers lifted themselves into the sky in a feeble effort to draw attention.

The wind cut through my coat as I walked back to the empty hostel, and I was ready to call it a night, Christmas Eve or not. Just as I was about to mount the stairs to my room, the hostel manager called out to me from several rooms away. I followed the sound of his voice through the dining area, past the kitchen, and into a dimly lit apartment. The manager introduced me to his girlfriend, who greeted me with a smile. On the dining room table was a simple feast, their Christmas Eve dinner, which they invited me to share. Candlelight shone through bottles of red table wine and glazed the food with the sheen of plenty.

They had already begun eating, but I quickly caught up, not realizing until then how hungry I was. The food was warm and filling, and the wine lit up my insides. As we ate, the hostel manager and his girlfriend nuzzled each other, comfortable with my being there, and I wished I knew more French so that we could talk. As it was, I thanked my hosts as best I could and wished them "*Joyeux Noël.*"

Later that night, as I lay in my chilly room, it struck me that I had been the object of pity – a solitary young American alone on Christmas Eve. But I didn't feel at all sorry for myself. I was glad to be on my own, away from family, away from teachers, roommates, and friends. I clung to the idea that for once I was finally living out my own script. I had wanted to see things sharply, feel things strongly, decide what I thought without someone telling me what to think. Now I was doing it, and had been touched by two strangers' invitation to share a meal.

Perhaps I had done the hostel manager and his girlfriend as much good as they did me, staving off the strangeness of a Christmas Eve outside their usual routines. I'll never know. On that Christmas Eve, given food better than I could provide for myself, and human company I didn't have to defend myself from or entertain, I accepted the social contract, and discovered that I was willing to be part of the human family.

The next morning, I gathered my things into my backpack and walked out into a sunny, windless day a little warmer than the day before. By that night, I made it to the tiny fishing village of Cassis, where on a headland covered in grass still green, I looked down onto the hammered steel of the Mediterranean, sun pouring down on the white mountains behind me and the calm sea all before me. Happy to be experiencing this moment alone, I was not lonely in the least. Why should I be? The night before, I had been taken in.

HARRY ROLNICK IS A WIDELY
TRAVELED WRITER WHO NOW FINDS
HIMSELF BACK HOME IN AMERICA AND
LIVING IN NEW YORK CITY.

RETSINA ROAD

HARRY ROLNICK

When reminiscing about hitchhiking through Greece, I realize it's the food I miss the most. Town markets would supply me with bags of olives, crumbly goat cheese, perhaps a flaky spanakopita (spinach pie). So many memorable flavors. However, for better or worse, my main memory harks from the island of Aegina, where I was baptized into the ritual of retsina. Certain comestibles stand out in the memory for their very ghastliness upon first consumption. Thailand's *durian*, Chinese sea cucumber and Japanese *nato*. And the retsina of Aegina. I speak of the resin peeled off pine trees, smashed into alcohol, left to vegetate for a few weeks like an errant child standing in a corner, and finally served in great grayish glasses to men of the sea and the islands. I speak of the retsina served on Aegina, poured from bottles with no labels, not poured smoothly but with chunky amber-brown globules, one of which was served to me.

No liquor this, but a torture of fermented tar, the alcohol biting the tongue, the resin sticking to the upper mouth, the odorous brew, rather than being swallowed, clinging to the throat like a leech before dropping down into the screaming gullet.

"Well?????" said Nicholas, my host in the taverna, waiting for my reaction.

"Delicious," I said. "Absolutely scrumptious." And then I gagged, not for telling a lie, but because the retsina had made

GREECE

44

a sudden jump back into the throat as if to escape, an alcoholic incubus ready for a night out.

I swallowed again, and again expressed my appreciation. But no more words were needed. Already, another unlabeled carafe was pulled from the shelf, a large dusty rag was slapped against the glass. Then the cork was pulled away.

"Another," said Nicholas. It was a command. The brownish liquor glared at me. Nicholas glared at me.

"To your health," he said.

"Thanks for the blessing," I said. And down went the retsina. With the second gulp, my inhibitions gave out, and I asked the inevitable.

"Who in hell . . . ?"

Nicholas gazed at me and poured out another glass. He was waiting for the sentence to be finished, but I had forgotten the question. Then it came.

"Who on earth invented this?"

Nicholas translated for the others now gathering around and filling up from the carafe. Nicholas had no answer, but one fisherman rattled away in some ancient Attic language, and it came out that retsina was – in his words – a mistake, an accident.

With the fourth carafe of retsina, I found my legs pushing off the floor and my body falling to the floor. Others in the taverna laughed (I was laughing too, of course), and my legs and body were put back together. I faced the retsina again. Nuts and honey and a paper-thin pastry were also pushed into my mouth.

Next I was hoisted upon shoulders, thrown into the back of a truck and taken to an old barn where music was playing. The barn had no lights. Just a few candles burning. And the music? It was called *rembetika* and was like retsina: sour, loud, unpalatable, jumpy in rhythm. I began to whirl with the music. I fell and was helped up by many arms. A dose of retsina kept me awake. The brew resembled jellied vodka spiked with razor blades. No carafe this time. The retsina was wheeled over in an old oak barrel and ladled into my glass.

Some of the older men simply went to sleep, but others insisted on dancing, and I danced with them. I suppose I danced with them.

It all became a clamorous dream in the darkness, as my arms were held up and one slow foot went in front of the other. I must have fallen a dozen times, but soon a group of us was dancing out to the port, where boats bobbed under the half-moon. Dancing on the port, walking nowhere, with shouts and music. I was a young zombie meandering along the quayside, with a concertina player following, his notes as wayward as my legs.

And that was all I remembered. The next morning I woke on a bed in a bare little room. I had been well looked after; apparently my own clownish excesses an entertainment to people who love to be entertained.

ROBERTA BEACH JACOBSON LEFT
CHICAGOLAND FOR A EUROPEAN VAC-
ATION IN 1974 AND NEVER RETURNED.
SHE MAKES HER HOME ON A REMOTE
GREEK ISLAND.

CAN YOU FIND THE FLUSHER

ROBERTA BEACH JACOBSON

Anyone who has visited Germany for longer than a few hours will have experienced the complexities of the dreaded German toilet system. *What's the big deal*? you say. *Just flush it!*

Flush it HOW? If there's a cord, chances are you pull it. The same applies to ropes, chains and wires. The challenge for you, my friends, is about to begin. Allow me to lead you down these steps to a typical public bathroom. Single file please. No passing on the stairway. Remember, this is Germany, the land of too-muchness when it comes to rules. Keep to the right. We'll assemble in that room down in the *keller – die toilette*.

The first thing you'll notice about German public bathrooms is the lack of heat. They're 32 degrees Fahrenheit, all year round, so don't go searching for any "hot seat" in here.

Next, notice these vending machines by this wall. German toilet tissue is definitely worth a mention. A tiny packet costs you anywhere from twenty cents up. Think you're getting the good stuff then, right? Ha. What you just purchased is the sandpapery, scratch-your-glasses-so-think-twice-if-you're-considering-using-it-elsewhere kind of toilet paper. Should have brought your own.

Next, you'll be put to the real test. With absolutely no prior instructions, you are expected to play the "find the flusher" game. Set the clocks, please. Okay, is it a metal button that

GERMANY

you attack with the toe of your right shoe? *No!* Tick, tick, tick. Could it be that rusty chain or twisted wire up there? *Nein!* Tick, tick, tick. Don't panic, just explore. You'll get it. What about an electronic switch in the corner? A sliding panel of some sort? A search behind the paper roll holder turns up as empty as the dispenser itself.

The crowd out there must be getting annoyed. You can hear their impatient sighs. What have you been doing for so long? Maybe there's some sort of sensor near the base? Somewhere, there *has* to be a way to flush!

Tick, tick, tick. The tourists in line are growing increasingly irritated, and you glance at the half-open window (just what you need in this already freezing room), hoping to spot something on the windowsill to unlock the mystery. Then, a sharp knock at your stall door disrupts your concentration.

You want so desperately to win this game. Head spinning, you sit back down. It seems your years of study of multicultural issues, and even physics, failed to prepare you for something this monumental. In utter despair, you whisper, "Open sesame." Zilch.

It seems the much-anticipated flush is just not going to happen. Yet another tourist will have to admit to being a total failure at German adaptation. In complete frustration, you bang your head against the metal door.

WHOOOOOOOOOOSH!

CHAPTER 2

YOU GET WHAT YOU PAY FOR

Rorie Brophy

be warned !

When asked by a friend to pick olives and prune olive trees . . . Refuse!!! (with violence if necessary)

As olive picking doesn't feature highly in a normal Irish upbringing, I was misled into believing that it involved some gentle outdoor work with lots of laying around under the shade of ancient olive trees drinking red wine and discussing Spanish poetry with good-natured locals while olives fell like autumn leaves into a waiting basket . . . (I had imagined the locals to be comely peasant girls . . . but I digress . . .)

I did not intend to spend the day doing hard labor under a blazing sun, hitting a tree with a stick to remove olives that are welded to the branch with such determination that one could swing off an individual olive with no danger of it separating from its parent tree!

Nor did I realize that I would be required to donate several liters of blood to giant insects thought to be extinct 65 million years ago . . . but which are actually alive and well and thriving on the rich Irish blood they have obviously acquired a taste for. They seemed utterly disinterested in Spanish blood . . . a fact I mentioned several times to the apparent amusement of the locals.

I am just out of the shower . . . I think my drain is now blocked with the dried blood, crushed insects and assorted olive debris that one acquires on this hellish activity.

I have six beers in the fridge which I am now required to drink for medicinal purposes.

I have removed from my little book the names of all friends who own or are suspected of owning olive trees. With friends like that . . .

AFTER HER TRAVELS IN EASTERN
EUROPE, KATHERINE WAS INSPIRED
TO JOIN THE PEACE CORPS IN
GUYANA, SOUTH AMERICA, WHERE SHE
WORKED WITH YOUNG WOMEN FOR TWO
YEARS. SHE IS NOW A SPECIAL
NEEDS YOGA TEACHER AND FREELANCE
WRITER LIVING IN BROOKLYN, AND IS
WORKING ON A SERIES OF STORIES
ABOUT HER LIFE IN GUYANA.

ONE MORE STORY TO TELL

KATHERINE JAMIESON

Recovering from Poland (severe Warsaw, poignant Kraków), you arrive by train in Prague on a windy March afternoon. Your body has begun to mold to the hard, red Polish train benches where you attempted sleep for two nights with your four companions, crossways and longways, to the rhythm of snores. The plush lime-green seats on the Austrian train mildly revived you and when hot chocolate arrived, unbidden and *gratis*, you took it as a sign you were heading in the right direction. Crossing borders in the night, woken to have a train pictograph stamped in your passport – you don't realize it yet, but you have reached the pinnacle of your journey, entering a city already more vivid to you, more alive than anywhere else you have traveled on this continent.

You are full of Eastern Europe, full of a sense of being somewhere your parents, most everyone you know really, have never been. The only advice they could offer was to bring toilet paper. Western Europe is balustrades and flying buttresses, stained glass and sepulchers. It is decadent and glorious, but has a tramped-upon feeling, as if the best of it was long ago buried under the ground you walk on today. Eastern Europe rises up from itself suddenly, forces you back in the wind, calls to you in sounds you do not identify as language, scowls at you from behind corners. It is dirtier than Italy, less precise than Switzerland, lacks the refinement of France, uncharted

PRAGUE

51

in your schoolish mind filled with encyclopedia images of the Eiffel Tower and London Bridge. Eastern Europe throws its history at you, and doesn't care if it hits you in the face or the stomach. It has a story to tell, about what can be forgiven and what never will be, and it wants to make sure you hear it, and remember it.

Ac–com–mo–da–tion!! Ac–com–mo–da–tion!! The plump, gray-haired women call to you, stressing each syllable of this formal, seemingly foreign word. *Ac–com–mo–da–tion!!* Ending with an upswing, a question, an irresistible offer of beds and shelter from this biting wind. A real Czech apartment! Your ragtag, under-dressed band tramps after its new landlady who offers an apparently good rate in crude English for her centrally located flat. Centrally heated as well, you hope.

Her apartment is located several streets behind the statue of a behemoth on a horse, vanquisher of an unknown battle. This mysterious, majestic rider is your North Star in Prague, your anonymous Polaris signaling the path homeward, up the dusty stairs to fall into bed each night, your eyes starry, belly full of fried cheese. He towers over you as you begin your wandering days through winding, cobblestone streets, past Byzantine churches, topsy-turvy cemeteries, cafés and bridges. All of it covered lightly in a coating of airborne pollution, giving the sense that if you were only to find a Brillo pad big enough to scratch the surface of Prague a little harder, you would find beneath a city of gold.

You have been in Eastern Europe long enough to hear of its mythic marvels and horrors, toilet paper being the least of it. Gypsies who throw babies at you and steal your wallet when you reach for the child. The Yellow Brick Road in Bulgaria, vampires in Romania, mermaids in Warsaw. But from all these stories you could never have guessed at what is now before your eyes. Prague is the first jewel you have ever seen up close – no glass window, no *Don't touch*! Prague salutes you at every corner, its mosaics and arches, its castle sitting above your head like a new moon. You rest in the shadows of statues, wander through graveyards, drink the real Budweiser. You get drunk, you get sober, but it's all the same, day after day, postcard after postcard – you can't believe this beauty.

You are sightseeing like a mad fiend, walking and walking far beyond the metro stops, beyond the castles, as if you are a newly landed explorer pushing the boundaries of your territory. But Prague eggs you on, because there is always something else to uncover – synagogues, tapestries, details on buildings that seem to be just buildings until you examine them closer, realizing the gargoyles and mermaids, the queens and dragons are all telling you a fantastic story about a different time and place, and you are now there.

You are fat and full of beauty and rich food and the unlikeliness of your camaraderie with fellow astonished travelers – three Americans and one Bermudan formerly acquainted primarily with Western Europe – but now residing, albeit transiently, in Prague, Czech Republic. You frequent extravagant coffee shops together, waxing poetic on waves of postcards, and you spend nothing, nothing! Because this is the other magic of Eastern Europe: where several hundred dollars earned you millionaire status in Poland, the zloty stretching the nylon on your money belts thick over your waist – your money means more here. Nothing costs anything.

So the truth is, dreams are dreams and life is life, and although both must end, dreams, as a rule, must end sooner. Your little band floats through Prague in a cultural bubble, not understanding, nor caring really, what is happening around you that you yourself are not making happen. The language is impenetrable, the gestures a murky mystery. Eventually, Prague decides she wants to know something about you.

One night you all stay home, tired of being out all the time, and you decide to cook. Thick, white noodles, plates and plates of them, and some concoction of tomato sauce with a lone vegetable you located in the market – broccoli perhaps? Beer. Bread. And chocolate, still intact from Birmingham, Cadbury's home. The night is progressing as all the others have in past weeks. Tipsy and brimming with pasta, you and your friend, another woman, venture downstairs. Out of your little apartment, down the dusty, gray stairs of this ancient old building, you step outside without shoes, and call up to your friends above you.

And then, out of nowhere, Prague approaches you. She comes in the form of a middle-aged, swollen, inebriated man who begins to ask you loud questions in Czech. You look at your friend, rather amazed that you have been noticed and addressed, and you both raise your arms in a shrug. *Sorry, don't understand.* The man talks louder, gesticulating vigorously, a lot of energy and – you can't imagine why – anger.

Sorry, you murmur in your own pathetic tongue, as useless as a cat's meow. *What do you want*, you ask, *we don't understand*, and you make a face of complete ignorance, which incites him more. Your conversation during this time is immeasurably complicated by the fact that while in your language "no" means "no," in Czech "no" means "yes." And thus, in response to your queries and pleas, your logical explanations for why you are standing in your socks in the lobby of a building you have rented from a woman you met in a train station, you hear what sounds like, "*Nooooooo!!*" (slurred Czech words and syllables, expletives) . . . "*Nooooooo!! Policii!!*" (Czech, Czech, Czech) . . . "*Policii!!*"

Finally, some communication, though of course not what you had hoped for. *Okay, okay, sorry we're going upstairs,* you say and quickly turn to make the ascent. A hand goes up. "*Pazport!*"

What? you ask. *Are you kidding? We can't give you our passports, we need those to travel to Hungary, Romania, home . . .*

"*Pazport!!*" Bravely your friend breaks free from the policeman's grip and runs up the stairs, leaving you with him for a mercifully short time in which he manages to communicate that he thinks both you and she are prostitutes. She gathers the rest of your group, who have been blissfully unaware of the international incident brewing just floors below them, and grabs your shoes. By the time your friends arrive, you have begun to wonder where in the world you are exactly and how you got to this God-forsaken place – people who drink all the time, being arrested on suspicion alone – these people are communists! Despair and reality begin to set in, all at the age of twenty, when it seems like vastly too much to think about, particularly after a full day of traipsing, and several shots of Becherovka.

A long evening ensues, beginning with a short trip to the police station which is conveniently located across the street. Here you are greeted by a rather young and startled-looking policeman. You stand in a holding cell, then a phone call is made and the phone is handed to you. The voice – female, in heavily German-accented English – wants to know what has happened. You explain, sounding indignant yet apologetic. It then becomes clear that perhaps your accommodations matron was not acting fully within the bounds of Czech law when she rented her place to you at, what you now realize, were very inflated rates.

You are released to go back home (across the street), feeling rather sobered. Thoughts edge toward your consciousness that you are a bit naïve, and perhaps even slightly arrogant – a wealthy American in a region that is, after all, recovering from decades of isolation and repression. Even deeper, you recognize that the bias of all travelers is also yours: that the whole reason this place is important to you, the whole reason that it even *exists* for you is because *you are here right now.* Otherwise you more or less don't care.

These fragments of thoughts are shunted to the back of your young mind, as you begin to revel in your evening's display of bravado. This is your world anyway! You had a scare, but you survived, met the challenge head on. You pack your bags the next day and board the train to Budapest with some really excellent photos and, yes, one more story to tell.

WILLIAM SUTTON GREW UP IN CENTRAL
SCOTLAND. RELIABLE REPORTS NOW
PLACE HIM IN BRAZIL, WHERE HE IS
PROBABLY TEACHING ENGLISH, PLAYING
THE UKULELE, AND DRINKING TOO
MUCH COFFEE.

THE DELINQUENTS OF MÁLAGA

WILLIAM SUTTON

It was a gamble from the start. As we sailed into Málaga after two
weeks slumming around Morocco, my friend and I agreed to split
up. He wanted to track down some girl from Madrid he'd once met
in a pub. I needed a lift straight back to Scotland.

I planned to catch a British truck off a cargo ship. Dutch would
do. Or even Danish. Once in a while the companies clamp down
and ban freeloaders, but mostly they're glad of the company.
Problem was, the next boat wasn't due for two days.

What harm could there be in spending a couple of nights in
Málaga, rather than heading pointlessly inland? It looked like a
charming little port, with the haze from the Mediterranean rising
over its hills. If only I hadn't wanted to see where Picasso was
born, I would never have met Joachim and his band of roustabouts.

I spotted a bed and breakfast with a smiling *matrona* and
reasonable rates. But my backpack was light – even with a
Moroccan carpet crammed inside it – so I decided to head straight
for Picasso's birthplace. I was inquiring at the information
kiosk when Joachim and Pritta overheard my infantile
Spanish.

"Come and stay with us," said Joachim gallantly. He was
fortyish and looked like a marooned pirate.

I was won over by their smiles and ability to speak
English. My friend and I had kept to ourselves in Morocco,

SPAIN

56

following a particularly bad carpet day in Tetouan. But back on European soil, surely I could relax and meet some locals.

"It's not the greatest house," Pritta admitted. Younger and blond, she was pleasantly ungainly in her jeans and leather jacket. "The roof rains–"

"But it's home," Joachim laughed.

I took them for students, picturing a poky apartment and dishes piled high in the sink.

Joachim bought red wine and Coke, mixing them and optimistically calling the result sangria. As late afternoon drew in, I shared a drink with Tonio, all bulging muscles, Gippe, with a long scarred face, and Jaime, an old sea dog. I should have been alarmed to see them crumble aspirin into their drinks, but that first night I was up for anything. We sat in the square, drinking, while the miraculous parade unfolded around us.

It was late when we finally stumbled up the dark hill beneath the city's castle. Below us, derelict houses tumbled back down towards the harbor. We clambered over a tiny breach in the wall, scrambled across a roof, and swung ourselves in through a crumbled doorway.

It was then that I realized my new companions were squatters.

Too drunk to care, I crawled into my sleeping bag as Tonio began to look through my stuff.

"Don't worry," Pritta smiled, lugging my pack out of sight. "I'll make him put everything back."

I woke in the night, shivering. They'd pulled my sleeping bag off me. Searching for Pritta, my protector, all I could see were stars gleaming through the holes in the roof. In the early hours of the morning, I heard her voice and called out, frightened and angry.

She apologized. The boys were drunk. With her bright-eyed shrug, I believed her.

We hurried out of the house before daylight, as the building was condemned. I tried to focus on the route, but my befuddled head couldn't take anything in. Joachim led the way, reassuring me that my stuff couldn't be safer. Back at the square, the police rounded us up to check our papers.

They weren't students, of course. The most fitting word for them I heard as I tugged my passport from my money belt.

"What," the police sneered, "are you doing with these delinquents?"

Pritta was standing close by. If I begged to be rescued, at best I'd escape and lose my things. At worst the police would leave me at the mercy of these criminals, so I said nothing.

"We are thieves, yes," Pritta told me winningly, emerging from a church with handfuls of coins. "But we won't steal from you."

Before I'd headed off for Europe, my father had offered me some advice. The suggestion I just couldn't accept was to start regularly reading newspapers; I figured I could catch up on important events when I got back home. But I did take a couple of things on board: if mugged, give them the money; I also accepted his fifty-pound note, zipping it into my wallet's secret pocket.

The few possessions I had on me seemed hugely precious. Wallet. Camera. Money belt. But not my harmonica. I'd played it a little earlier that morning, but Tonio had wrapped his lips around it and strolled off. To a pawnshop, I supposed. He returned with the first of the day's wine and pills, and it was in good spirits that they led me to the soup kitchen for lunch.

My mind spun into overdrive, inventing plan after plan to outwit them, find my rucksack, and vanish without a word.

Making an excuse, I slipped off, and heart racing, found my way back to the castle road above the derelict houses.

But I couldn't find the path. Everything looked different: there were no roofs to scramble across, no disheveled doorways to slip through.

I walked up and down, growing increasingly anxious, sure they would send someone to find me. I pictured the light in Tonio's eyes.

But what was the worst they could do? Kill me? Rape me? Walk away now and I'd be in one piece. But my stuff! I'd be abandoning it, and through *such* stupidity on my part.

Or I could return to them and bide my time, stay sober till they led me back, then tiptoe out to freedom. Was it worth such a long shot? The Walkman was replaceable. The carpet I could leave. But there were my contact lenses. My address book. My journal!

I decided to gamble.

Back at the square, I took up the casual manner that carried me through that long, long evening. How unexpectedly the stakes had risen – from the simple decision to wait for a truck, to this.

As they were sinking into drunkenness, I went over my plan again and again in my head. Snapping photos casually, like we were friends having a good time, I made sure to get a good shot of each of them, brewing vengeful dreams in my heart. I'd put these harmonica villains behind bars.

That second night seemed colder. I started to panic: if we all walked back together, I wouldn't stand a chance. What might become of me beneath those dark castle walls? When Joachim asked if I'd like to go home early, I gasped with relief.

"Just us," Pritta nodded. Perfect.

Even as it happened, it didn't seem surprising. Halfway there, Joachim tugged me from the path into the darkness beneath a little stone bridge. I knew, even then, it could have been much worse. I remember none of what he said. But I recall he held the knife against me in four different places.

Pritta stayed silent. Maybe she was embarrassed. Somehow, I was strangely impressed. What a tidy game she had played, engaging my trust, shrugging off my fears.

Notions passed through my head to run for it, lash out, grab the knife and drag them to the police. But my father's voice echoed in my head: you can get another credit card but not another face.

I gave Joachim my wallet and traveler's checks; he took the cash and my camera too. I begged forlornly to keep the film, but he told me to run away and not to make a sound. As I reached the path, he called out and threw something towards me. I snatched it up – my wallet – and ran.

The police were bored.

I made everything clear. I knew where the thieves were, could point out the hideaway where my goods were stashed (roughly). A raid might unearth a mountain of loot.

They gave me an insurance form to write down what had been lost.

"Stolen!" I insisted.

The sunlit city which had seemed so welcoming when I skipped innocently off the boat, now oozed threat and melancholy. That night, I slept in the top bunk of a doss house, my dreams lurid and unquiet.

The next day, the British Consulate did not offer to fly me home at the earliest opportunity, and it took some persuading to let me phone home.

Short on sympathy, my parents just wanted to know how I was going to get back to the United Kingdom. I should have been waiting in the port for my Anglo-Danish trucker, but a mammoth bus ride sounded infinitely better.

Of course, the fifty-pound note was still secreted in my wallet. Exulting in my riches, I spent hours in a department store over coffee and *The Times*. My father had been right: if I hadn't relied on novels to learn about the world, perhaps I'd have avoided a disaster such as this.

Then I remembered my dream from the dosshouse. I'd been back in the thieves' lair, and could clearly recall exactly how to get in, the little breach in the wall marking the path between the houses. I'd even seen it the day before, when I'd been searching so desperately, but it had not registered.

I ran most of the way there. It was still daylight, and I figured they shouldn't be back until well after dark. Still, my heart thumped as I went up the castle road, past the place where they'd robbed me.

And there it was. Exactly as I'd dreamt.

Clambering over the breach and across the roof, I peered through the crumbled doorway. There, amongst the dust, dirt and exposed bricks, was a T-shirt. My T-shirt. And . . .

Nothing else.

Trembling with fear, I squeezed through a knocked-through wall and down stairs filthy with mold, towards an old wardrobe. I could hear a woman singing nearby, and the clanging of pots and pans. But there was nowhere to go.

Tugging at the wardrobe door, it finally opened to reveal an assortment of fresh-scented clothes, not the musty damp I had expected. There, between the shirts, I saw a light. Stepping through, it was another world: an immaculate bedroom with a double bed, fresh sheets and crisply plumped pillows. The Queen Bee's room.

My backpack's contents were spilled across the floor. No Walkman, but my contact lenses, address book and journal.

My mind swarmed with horrible thoughts of wrecking or setting fire to the room, but panic returned. I left my contact lens disinfectant pills, in the hope that the thieves would choke on their sangria, scrambled back onto the road, and headed straight to the bus station.

I've learned some more Spanish since then, mainly from girls in pubs, but I've never gone back to Málaga, or to Spain. I doubt I ever will.

MYRNA MCKEE IS A YANKEE JEWISH
PRINCESS HAPPILY MARRIED INTO
THE SOUTH MANY YEARS AGO. SHE
CALLS HER CAPTURED MOMENTS AND
VIGNETTES *PAINTING WITH WORDS*.

AT LEAST YOU HAVE A SEAT

MYRNA MCKEE

My roommate Cindy and I each had twenty-five dollars, a string
bag filled with provisions, and a tiny overnight bag, which con-
tained a change of underwear, pajamas, one dress, a pair of shoes
and a few cosmetics. Taped to our bags were signs that read,
Estudiantes a Madrid.

Suitably attired for the journey in sweaters and leather jackets,
we departed the Left Bank by metro to the last stop on the outskirts
of Paris. Without a map, we approached the edge of the highway
going south and stuck out our thumbs.

At once, a car driven by a lady stopped. "Where are you going?"
she inquired in English.

We pointed to the signs on our overnight bags.

Shaking her head in disbelief, she motioned for us to get in her
car. "Do you know the French word for *hitchhiking*?" Seeing the
blank looks on our faces, she laughed softly and said, "Poor
American babies. *Par auto stop* is the phrase you need to
know. And it's not at all European to stick one's thumb out."
The signal was to extend one hand straight towards the road
with all the fingers together, she explained.

Thirty minutes and forty miles later, our ears were full of
instructions: *Don't get into a car with more than one man in
it*, and *Be sure to be off the road by dark*. Our Samaritan
wished us good luck and left us on the side of the road. Later,

FRANCE

we discovered that the French never wish you good luck unless they really feel you're going to need it.

Our next ride was with an old man going, via Lyon, to San Sebastiàn – three hundred miles away near the border between France and Spain. This driver, Jacques, expected us to keep the conversation going, and Cindy was forced to carry most of the load. It was worth it. When we took from our string bags the bread and cheese for our lunch, Jacques explained in simple French that we were his guests. In the town of Beaujolais, we dined in a local café where Jacques insisted he pay for our meal. To be in France eating authentic food, to drink Beaujolais table wine in the town of Beaujolais – life couldn't get much better.

Back on the road, with Cindy in the front seat doing all our talking, I drifted off to sleep some time in the late afternoon. Next thing I knew we were in San Sebastiàn and it was dark.

Jacques insisted on taking us to his home where his wife Solange had supper waiting: bubbling homemade bean soup with crusty bread, Camembert, apples and wine. We could barely understand each other, but we ate, sang songs and drank wine. Cindy and I ended the evening tucked into a big feather bed by our generous hosts.

Solange woke us early the next morning with a breakfast tray containing two full bowls of hot chocolate, fresh warm bread, sweet butter and homemade fruit jam. After breakfast we said goodbye with hugs and kisses, and were sent off with a fully packed basket for lunch.

But sure enough, after so many miles, Lady Luck deserted us. A short way into our next ride, the car's engine threw a rod and we couldn't continue driving. After waiting by the side of the road for over an hour, a local bus to Madrid finally stopped and picked us up. It was old and rattled, glass was missing from all of the windows, and the unpainted wooden seats had been worn smooth by years of use. Amongst the numerous riders were two cases of squawking chickens, one old man holding a squirming pig in a sack, and three nuns praying over their rosary beads the entire time.

From the way we were dressed, it was obvious we were American. Our pants were probably considered "racy" and in bad taste amongst the flowing skirts and dresses around us. But this wasn't a problem. Even though no one understood a word of English, everyone on board was friendly and pleasant.

It was a slow ride. On a good stretch of road we got up to twenty miles an hour. Uphill was another story. We would all have to get off while the men helped push the bus to the top of the hill. Then we'd climb back in for the ride down.

When it came time for lunch, the bus driver parked by a stream. The women, all carrying huge baskets, spread sparkling white tablecloths on a grassy slope. We added the contents of Solange's plentiful basket to the picnic, which included crusty loaves of bread, wheels of hard cheese, hard-boiled eggs, ham, sausage, oranges, nuts and bottles of local wine. As we ate, the men smoked cigars and drank wine straight from the bottles. Two elderly men with harmonicas serenaded us all.

No one seemed too concerned about time. After an hour or so, all the passengers began to pick out a spot to lie down for a siesta. Shrugging our shoulders, we too settled down for the communal nap. At four o'clock the driver woke us, ready to continue the journey. After quickly gathering the remains of our picnic, we climbed back on board the bus.

It took twenty hours to travel the two hundred miles to Madrid. As we approached the outskirts of the city, the ancient bus gave a large shuddering bang, and with smoke pouring from its engine, it crawled to a stop.

Realizing that to wait would be futile, we picked up our luggage, found the subway with the help of our new friends, and bought two third-class tickets to downtown Madrid. Unfortunately, it was early morning rush hour and when our train eventually pulled into the station, what seemed like hundreds of third-class passengers were pushed into only one car. There was no room to move and barely enough to breathe.

Suddenly Cindy's face turned tomato red.

"Are you all right?" I asked.

"The man behind me has his hands on my butt and is cupping the cheeks," she sputtered. "What should I do?"

"I'd sit down if I were you," I told her, exhausted after our long trip. "At least you have a seat."

AFTER SEVERAL TRIPS TO EUROPE,
KATHY COUDLE KING NOW TEACHES
ENGLISH AND WOMEN'S STUDIES AT
THE UNIVERSITY OF NORTH DAKOTA.
HER FIRST NOVEL, *WANNABE*, IS
BASED ON HER EXPERIENCES GROWING
UP IN FLORIDA AND NEW JERSEY.

MY STINKY CHEESE NIGHT

KATHY COUDLE KING

Traveling by myself was a dream that had always both excited and scared me a little. I was not so fearful of all the horrible things that could happen to a woman by herself in a foreign country: rape, murder, being sold into slavery. No, I was afraid of much more scary stuff, like what direction to look when I ate dinner by myself. Could I have a beer in a bar if I wanted to, and not feel like a freak? It was a challenge I just had to put to the test. So, I pushed myself forward and organized my plane tickets, with a week scheduled to travel on my own before heading to a friend's wedding in Switzerland.

I highly recommend traveling by oneself from time to time – there are a lot of perks. Getting lost is so much better alone. In Amsterdam, when the streets spiral around and spit you out at a place you can't find on your torn and wrinkled map, there's no one to yell at you when you get the directions wrong. You can just pretend you meant to wind up where you did all along. And in the museums, you can take as long as you like in front of a work of art; there's no one breathing heavily, shifting from foot to foot, tugging at your sleeve to get you moving.

When I was in Amsterdam, my favorite adventure was the day I took a bike tour of the countryside. Again, this was something I could just decide to do without having to negotiate

AMSTERDAM

with anyone. A friendly guide took us through the wet landscape, and we visited a farm where Gouda cheese was made. The tour guide told us we could purchase the cheese and it would keep until we returned home. I bought two large wheels, put them in my trusty backpack and didn't think about them again until I returned to Amsterdam after my friend's wedding.

Before flying home, I planned to spend a few more days by myself to recover from the two weeks I'd survived with the bride-to-be. Talk about stressful – but that's another story.

The night before I was to fly out, I went into one of the pubs, now an expert at drinking by myself. (I brought along a notebook and pretended to be a journalist from the States, if anyone asked.) So there I was, drinking my *pils*, when along came a handsome man of Middle Eastern appearance. He wasn't turned off by my journalist stance but instead offered to accompany me to a disco. This sounded intriguing, so off we went to dance to Milli Vanilli at a packed club that was within walking distance.

We had a great time, and when I tell you the guy wanted to come home with me, I mean, *the guy wanted to come home with me*. He was from Algiers, and he was quite interested in hooking up with me in the United States. In fact, he'd thought we'd made a soul connection, and it was tough getting rid of him. Fortunately, when we got back to my youth hostel, it became clear that our little adventure had ended. I really lost patience with him when I realized I had missed the curfew at the hostel and the doors were locked, but it was then that my Algerian companion became a real friend. Speaking to the night caretakers in their native Arabic, he got one of them to unlock the door for me. I shook hands with my knight in shining armor and told him to look me up when he got to America.

It was quite late by this time, two or three in the morning. The hostel gently reverberated with the sounds of sleep. Slightly tipsy, I did my best to creep into my room without waking the other six or so residents. One of them looked up and gave me a scowl as I came in; another rolled over as I got into my bottom bunk, causing it to creak loudly.

Completely dressed, I dared only remove my sneakers. That's when the trouble began. I'd been wearing those tennis shoes for three weeks, most of the time without socks, and some days had gone by without taking a shower either, because it wasn't always convenient or because the hostel's facilities weren't always enticing. In any case, those sneakers of mine reeked. They stunk so bad that I was sure the guy who'd given me the dirty look when I walked in could smell them. They stunk so bad that I was certain everyone in the dorm room was going to wake up, and yell at me in many languages: *Get yourself and your smelly sneakers out of here!*

Stealthily, I sat up in bed, trying hard not to cause the springs to squeak. I picked up my sneakers and put them on the windowsill, figuring that the open window would allow the stench of my sneakers to blow out of the room. Good in theory, but wrong in practice. The wind that particular evening was blowing *into* the room. As I lay in my bed staring up at the bunk above me, great gusts of my sweat-soaked shoes filled the room. I cautiously sat up, grabbed the sneakers, and crept to the adjoining shower area. I put my offending footwear in the sink, lathered them with soap, stuck my head close to their inner soles, and inhaled. Not great, but definitely better.

Returning to the dorm room, all was quiet, and I pushed my now-soaking sneakers deep beneath the bed. In the process, my hand bumped my backpack. I'd taken a risk leaving it there while I'd been out drinking beer with my Algerian friend. Suddenly, I had a horrible feeling that I shouldn't have. Carefully, still trying to be quiet, I slid the zipper open to see if anything had been stolen. It was mostly dirty clothes, as I carried my passport, plane tickets, and money in a hip pouch, but you never know, someone might have been desperate for my dirty laundry. At this point I would have *given* them my sneakers. But no, nothing was missing: all my clothes and souvenirs were accounted for, the program from my friend's wedding was there, the ticket stubs from the museums I'd attended to prove I'd gone to them, and the cheese I'd purchased three weeks before. Yet the offending sneaker smell was more acute than ever. I stuck my head into the backpack to get a better whiff, and – oh! It was awful. The cheese! It dawned on me at last.

I reached in to grab one of the wheels of Gouda, but my fingers sunk into the spoiled mess, protected only by wax paper. The heavy cheese had sunk to the bottom of my backpack, and I'd kept stuffing dirty laundry on top of it, failing to realize that it wasn't my clothes that were so offensive, after all.

What to do with it? If I put it in the room's trash can, the stench would surely wake up the entire hostel. I had to get the cheese out of there. Up again, I went to the bathroom with my backpack. I can only imagine what the other occupants of the room must have thought. I found a garbage can as far from the sleeping area as possible, and dropped the squishy, moldy, stinky cheese into it with a solid *thud-thud*.

After washing my hands, I crept back to my bed once more and lay staring up at the sagging mattress above me. I could still smell it – that horrible, wrinkle-your-nose, pinch-your-nostrils odor was wafting out from beneath the shower stall, floating into the room. I lay there in fear, eyes wide, waiting for one of my bunk mates to jump up and scream.

Wide awake until dawn I waited, until finally, as the night sky began to turn pink, I rose and grabbed my few belongings, including the still-wet sneakers. Without shower or toilet, I headed for the airport. At customs they asked me if I had any perishables. I could honestly say no, but I think the scent of old cheese was still clinging to me because they went through my backpack anyway. The customs officer narrowed his eyes, and gestured with his head that I could leave. Slinking away in my squishy sneakers and a cloud of stench, I know I had obviously given new meaning to the phrase "ugly" American.

IN EIGHT YEARS OF TRAVEL WRITING
FOR LONELY PLANET, DANI VALENT HAS
WORKED ON OVER A DOZEN GUIDES TO
DESTINATIONS ON FOUR CONTINENTS.
SHE STILL LOVES COMING HOME TO
MELBOURNE, AUSTRALIA, WHERE SHE
DREAMS ABOUT MAKING THE PERFECT
CRÈME BRÛLÉE AND PLAYING AUSSIE
RULES FOOTBALL FOR CARLTON.

FIERCE HOSPITALITY

DANI VALENT

Waiting for a connecting bus in a nowhere town, I went to linger over a tea in a grimy *lokanta*. The waiter (assisted by assorted friends and regulars) stationed himself at my table and insisted that I miss my bus and stay another day. They promised a tour, a family to stay with, inspected my ticket, assured me they could change it and sent someone out to buy celebratory baklava. Someone else ran out spontaneously and came back ten minutes later with a massive muddy watermelon. I explained that I couldn't possibly stay, that I had friends waiting for me at the other end, a schedule to keep. A cell phone was offered to me. "Call your friends! Tell them you will come in two days." The friendliness was fierce. The host instinct seemed to explode out of these people as soon as they knew I was a visitor. They had hospitality, and by golly, they weren't afraid to wield it. After a couple of hours of me insisting I would catch my bus, it eventually arrived and they waved me off sadly. My watermelon rolled up and down the aisle for the entire journey.

TURKEY

LIZA PERRAT IS AN AUSTRALIAN
FREELANCE WRITER, ENGLISH TEACHER
AND TRANSLATOR LIVING IN LYON,
FRANCE. SHE SPENT HER TWENTIES
BACKPACKING THROUGH EUROPE AND
ASIA, AND MET HER FRENCH HUSBAND
IN THAILAND THIRTEEN YEARS AGO.

SLOW BUS TO FETHIYE

LIZA PERRAT

I blame it all on too much Turkish wine, and trusting Mustapha.

With lank hair, greasy skin and a girth that had housed one too many kebabs, Mustapha was not a great advertisement for his restaurant, but we went in anyway. In the tiny village of Pamukkale, there wasn't much of a choice.

Making inroads into our chicken kebabs, accompanied by a bottle of tart local red wine, we relaxed on the terrace. Bathed in moonlight, Pamukkale – a creation of white calcium deposits, or travertines, from the ancient hot springs of Hierapolis – stretched into the spectral night. Brilliant stalactites hung from the edges of pools and steps; the silence only broken by spring waters cascading over the slopes.

Mustapha chatted and joked with us, sitting a tad too close for comfort. Switching easily between American, Australian and European slang affirmed the years of experience dealing with travelers under his straining belt.

"You want to catch a bus to Fethiye?" he inquired, bird eyes blinking away tears of sweat.

"Yes, but we want a nice bus, with air conditioning," I said.

"No problem," he smiled reassuringly. "Come with me."

Tired from slipping over terraces of accumulated limestone sediment amidst throngs of noisy tourists, we were not up to fussing over a bus ticket. And there wasn't any reason

TURKEY

71

to think this bus wasn't going to be like the others we'd taken across Turkey: spotless, air-conditioned Mercedes, with bucket seats and impeccably dressed hosts offering cup after cup of Turkish coffee. Thus, we merrily accompanied Mustapha to a dim office to purchase our tickets.

At the Denizli bus station, business was booming. Long lines of travelers waited for transport to all corners of Turkey and beyond. Dark-haired men shouted unintelligibly as women sweltered in silence under layers of clothing, toddlers with gold earrings clinging to their skirt folds. The bus exhaust snorted pollution into the sticky morning air, but we didn't care, envisioning the turquoise Mediterranean waters we'd soon be cooling off in.

And then we saw our bus. It was not sporting a Mercedes logo and the air conditioning must have been out of action for decades. I think it was white, but the bodywork was more rust than paint, so it was hard to tell. I glanced aghast at the narrow, bald tires and hoped it was some sort of mistake.

"This bus doesn't look like it could go three miles, let alone one hundred and eighty!" I wailed. But since there were so many people waiting, we merely cursed Mustapha and shoved our way on board to claim a seat, all pretences at politeness flying out of the grimy windows.

We were soon swimming in sweat on the vinyl seats and grabbing hold of each other around hairpin bends so as not to slide off onto the squalid floor. Men chatted amicably, and several families and a goat stood for the whole six-hour trip.

Someone wanted to get on or off every few minutes. Since the speedometer never rose above ten kilometers per hour, we barely had to slow down for disembarking passengers. A few windows begrudgingly opened a crack and the August heat blasted in.

After two and a half hours, the bus lurched to a groaning halt. Refreshments stop, we imagined. The thermometer read 90 degrees and we noted an absence of trees or any other shade.

Without thinking, I ate some crisps: a personal morale booster in the bleakest of situations. What a mistake. Back on the dusty road, my parched throat craved cold water. Looking sadly at the inch of water jiggling in yesterday's water bottle, I decided that hot water was better than no water. We shared the precious drops.

With its gearbox groaning, the bus lurched up unpaved mountain paths. Some lucky people snored, heads wobbling, but we – seated alongside the noisy gearbox – could only stare at the arid, unwelcome expanse of trees and mountains, as thirsty and isolated as us.

Six hours into the trip, the bus began to smell like sardines forgotten in the sun. We had finally reached Fethiye.

"Hallelujah!" someone cried weakly.

Our vehicle coughed and died between two elegant coaches that had also just arrived from Denizli.

"I don't believe it," I murmured wearily.

Our driver descended without a word and fled into anonymity, avoiding a busload of black looks.

"At least we made it," my friend consoled.

And later, submerged in the heavenly coolness of Ölüdeniz, the receding waves managed to wash away all dust, sweat and regrets.

WILL BRADSHAW'S STORY "CITY OF
POETS" APPEARS EARLIER IN THIS
ANTHOLOGY.

SAINTS' STATION, BARCELONA

WILL BRADSHAW

We are running. Running through the train station, through the doors,
out into the warm Spanish night. I'm sure they are going to kick my ass.

I hadn't felt their eyes on me when I'd stepped off the train, but
they must have been watching, must have taken notice of my
clothes, the way that I moved. I took notice of the city only, wondered where I'd find a room.

I found a number in my address book and squeezed into a phone
booth, kneeling against my backpack and pressing my daypack into
the wall with my legs. Suddenly, there was a tap on my shoulder. I turned to find a man staring at me, saying something
that I could not understand. When I hung up the phone, my
daypack fell to the ground.

I asked the man what he wanted. He looked at me confused,
spoke again, then began to make writing signs with his hands.
I offered him my pen. No, he shook his head, but kept jabber-
ing on, still shaking his head *no*. Then suddenly three bodies
were pressing against me, too close. Everyone was talking,
but I couldn't understand a thing.

As I spun around, my eyes focused on one of the men:
short and well-built; dark, nearly black eyes set in an
unshaven face; dark skin, burnt by too much sun.

Then they were gone, as was my daypack.

74

"Shit!" I looked up to see the first man walking slowly away. I ran up to him and grabbed both of his shoulders, pushing him against the wall.

"*Dónde están sus amigos?*" I demanded.

But he said they weren't his friends, that he was alone. I understood perfectly. Sliding out of my grasp, he bolted away from me. I grabbed my phone card and address book, ready to follow. It was then that I noticed a police station on the opposite side of the concourse. I ran across and knocked on the door, but all was silent. My guy was near the exit now. I hurried down towards him, and stepped outside in time to see him board a bus.

Okay, okay, okay. What did I lose? Camera, coat, six rolls of film. Some batteries. My journal! Shit!

Bang, bang, bang. Back at the police station, someone was beating on the door with both fists. "*Heeeeewheeewww,*" he whistled. Bang, bang, bang. The door opened. The man lowered his voice, turned slightly, and I recognized the face I had seen before – dark, unshaven, with black eyes. It was him for sure, and he was pointing at me! Hurrying towards him, I racked my brains for the word for thief. *Ladrón.* That was it.

"*Dígale, dígale!*" Tell him, the man demanded in an Italian accent, pointing at the policeman. I stepped towards the cop.

"*Me han robado, y este hombre . . .*" I said, and the policeman nodded. Satisfaction at last.

"*No, tú. Yo. Me han robado.*" But what was this? The short man was now claiming that he himself was the victim, not me.

"*Perdón?*"

"*Me han robado!*" I have been robbed, he repeated, pulling out his wallet and pointing to places where cards were supposed to be.

He grabbed my backpack, peeling it from my shoulders and throwing it in the door to the police station with his own.

"*Venga,*" he said. Come.

Now we are running, out into the warm Spanish night. Turning a corner, we head down a spiral walkway and end up below the road, where apartments are stacked on apartments. A balding, shirtless man stands on the edge of the street.

"*Arriba*," he says before we ask, and points. At the corner is a dumpster, with a small car parked behind it. Two people are rummaging through a bag on the hood of the car.

"*Es mía.*" I run and grab it. The six rolls of film are there, so is the coat, the batteries and my Dictaphone. Still no journal. We run back to the shirtless man.

We need to call the police, I tell him, but he waves us back onto the road, telling us that he'll call himself, and that we should continue looking.

We jog back to the corner, turn right onto a shadowed street where houses and people and bars crowd every corner. There is a neon light for a pub in front of us, people crossing the road to go in. Just past the door to the pub, I see a pile of paper on the ground, glimpse something green and familiar. My maps, my book, my journal. Hallelujah.

But the camera is gone, as I knew it would be. Kicking at the ground, I cannot believe I have been such a fool, that the police cannot patrol an area twenty feet from the station.

We go around another corner, turn left, and end up in front of the shirtless man's apartment. The Italian man begins kicking at the bushes. When he thinks he sees something, he peers into the hedge, but it's never anything worthwhile. I try to help, but find only garbage.

The police arrive, and the short Italian guy pokes me: *Tell him.*

I say that we were both robbed at the station, and that there were three men. But the Italian shakes his head and holds up two fingers.

I tell the whole story as I believe it happened. My bag was taken in the train station. I have found a lot of my stuff, but the Italian has lost his passport, his credit cards, his money, everything.

The policeman nods. Then he opens the back door to the patrol car. The inside of the car reminds me of an oven that needs cleaning. The Italian man gets in behind me.

"*Dos hombres, correcto?*" The policeman asks as he slides into the passenger side.

"*Sí señor.*"

The Italian man wipes sweat from his forehead and whispers that I should tell them to open the windows.

We drive in and out of little side streets, dart past apartments, bars, hordes of people stumbling from one place to another in a haze, and everyone looks like the two thieves to me. I only saw the guy now beside me, but he claims he's a victim, too. We drive off the road, up onto the sidewalk, and back to the train station.

I walk inside to grab my backpack, and head across the hall to the bank of phones. Then there is a tap on my shoulder. I spin around too quickly and grab at the hand. It is my Italian companion.

"*Perdón.*"

The man asks if he can leave his bag with me while he goes to the bathroom. I nod, and lean against the wall between two phones, the Italian's bag resting on my feet. I watch the people who remain in the station. There are no more departures tonight. What are they still doing here? I glare at anyone who comes too close. Finally, the Italian comes back and asks if he can return the favor by minding my bag while I too go to the bathroom.

I peel my backpack off and set it by his feet, then wander into the bathroom, my daypack still strapped to my chest.

When I step out of the bathroom into the soft light of the station, the bank of phones is deserted. I spin in a circle, and run toward the booth where I left my bag with the Italian. I find a piece of paper underneath the phone. Scrawled across it in uneven letters is a single phrase:

Gracías por su bolsa. Thank you for your bag.

A NATIVE NEW YORKER, JIM EAGEN
SPENT HIS TWENTIES TRAVELING FAR
AND WIDE, LIVING AND PLAYING
MUSIC IN EASTERN EUROPE. WHEN NOT
ON THE ROAD, JIM, HIS WIFE ELLEN
AND THEIR TODDLER, BEN, SPLIT
TIME BETWEEN SAN FRANCISCO AND
ITHACA, NY. JIM'S LATEST BOOK
IS *FIRST PEOPLES: THE AYMARA OF
SOUTH AMERICA*.

THIS ISN'T THE GREYHOUND, IS IT?

JIM EAGEN

PRAGUE–BULGARIA

Despite the fact that revolution and war have tried to knock down Prague, it remains a place that looks more like a museum turned inside out than a major urban center. Visitors all know it as a magical city, full of life and wonder, where people come from all over the world, hoping to find inspiration for a work of art or, better yet, that cosmopolitan love so absent in places like Des Moines, Iowa, or Brighton, England. For two 23-year-olds from New York, the move to Prague a few months earlier provided an opportunity to write and become enraptured by the city's medieval charm. My friend Skay and I had similar desires – we knew the American job market was bankrupt and hoped life in Prague would be cheap, exciting and full of endless opportunity.

However, Prague had fast become overwhelmed with twenty-something Americans, much like us, all of whom thought they were writing the next *Farewell to Arms*. In a short time, too much talk, too much drinking and too many of the same faces had made Prague seem less exotic and much more irritating. Skay and I thought perhaps Bulgaria held some promise. We began asking around about going to this Balkan country on the Black Sea. The answers we heard most were "Why?" or "No one goes there."

Nonetheless, these answers fueled our fire. What better way to avoid the masses of Westerners than to head where none of them wanted to go? We had not met a single traveler who had been to Bulgaria, and no one seemed to know a thing about it, except one Canadian bartender who told us about a special bus. It went directly to Sofia, cost twenty-five dollars, and was leaving Monday afternoon from behind the National Museum.

It didn't take much effort to pack up our things and make arrangements to leave. We arrived a bit early at the bus stop, with backpacks in one hand and crisp American bills in the other. Cautiously walking up to buy a ticket from the young woman checking passports and passengers, it quickly became clear that something was not quite right. She paused, looked at our money, and said something in Czech that sounded like we were not allowed on the bus.

Before we could ask any questions, the bus driver rushed over, spoke tersely with her, and immediately assured us that everything was fine, taking our American dollars without even counting them. No ticket was issued, our passports were not checked and the woman in charge looked as confused as we were.

The next clue that something was a bit strange came when we boarded the bus. Our fellow passengers were all men. Dark-haired and in their early thirties, most had three-day-old growth on their faces and were wearing mirrored sunglasses. I hesitated, but Skay told me to act like I knew what was going on and take a seat near the rear. In a matter of minutes, the bus pulled away from the curb.

The first leg of the trip was uneventful. The other passengers mostly slept or kept fairly quiet. In fact, nobody seemed to talk at all. We read books and looked for castles tucked away in the countryside as the day faded.

The bus only made one stop, which I thought was near Szeged, along the Hungarian border with Romania. There we disembarked with the other men who were stepping out for a quick smoke. One particularly large guy was in the rest rooms at the same time as me, and I noticed he still had his shades on. When he looked down to flush the urinal, they slipped off and one of the lenses popped out as they hit the tile floor. He cursed in a language new to me, picked the piece up and continued back to the bus. "Serves him right," I thought. "Who's so cool that he needs to wear sunglasses at night?"

It was now after midnight and hard to see anything out of the windows; however, we could make out large military vehicles parked at road crossings, and even some tanks with soldiers in fatigues. "Odd," I thought. "Why the need for military presence after midnight? It must be a Romanian thing." I had heard much about the revolt of 1989 and the execution of the Romanian dictator Ceausescu. Perhaps this sort of policing was still needed years later.

As we approached passport control, more and more military personnel surrounded our bus. The heavy guns and helmeted soldiers glaring as we slowly passed made me uneasy. Skay was asleep, leaving me to fret in silence.

Then, the doors to the coach opened and a soldier carrying an assault rifle boarded. He asked for passports and began to check each passenger's, one by one. He joked with some of the passengers up front, which calmed me somewhat, but when he reached us, he took the documents without looking at our faces. He scanned our passports, paused and then looked up at us, eyes wide.

"*Americanskis!*" he shouted. "Very bad, very bad!" Our passports still in his hand, he bolted from the bus.

At this point, I decided that the passports were too important to watch disappear. I ran off the bus, following the soldier toward the control hut. But before my feet could hit the pavement, the bus driver yanked me back.

"It's okay. We wait for you. We will not leave you here," he promised me in surprisingly good English. "We wait here on Hungary side. Not going to Belgrade without you and your friend."

Belgrade? That's in Serbia. Weren't we heading through Romania? Who would take this route during the Balkans War? My nerves turned to nausea.

Shaking myself, I hustled over to the border control hut, searching for the soldier who had taken our documents. But the other soldiers played dumb, looking at me blankly when I asked where he'd gone. No one helped, even as I slumped over the counter, exasperated.

After ten minutes passed, I began to wonder if the bus driver really would wait. But what could I do? The guy with my passport dictated when I could go.

Finally, from a back room came the soldier grinning widely, our passports in hand. He approached the counter, took out a stamp and began to laugh.

"Just joking," he chuckled, filling out what looked like a visa. "Me hurt you? No way. I hurt you, Bill Clinton hurt me!" He erupted into laughter, along with the other soldiers within earshot, and handed me the passports back, along with transit visas, then disappeared into the back room once again.

Shaken and thoroughly confused, I jogged back to the bus. As I boarded, my welcome was like that of an Olympic athlete.

"Good job American!"

"Way to go U.S.A.!"

Skay sat smiling and once I climbed over his legs to my window seat, he began to fill me in.

"Hey, guess what? This isn't the Romanian border," he began. "It's the Serbian boarder. And these aren't just passengers going home to see their loved ones or visit Bulgaria – they're petty criminals! They got caught in the Czech Republic for small crimes: gunrunning, gambling, stuff like that. Mafia-type stuff. Now they're being deported to Bulgaria – that's where most of them are from."

At that moment, the big man I had encountered at the urinal leaned toward us from the seat across the aisle. "You guys big. Americans no wanted here. Everyone think you guys great," he said, pumping his fist to show his approval.

Our stupidity and lack of foresight was interpreted as bravado and swagger. No one on the bus realized that we were looking for a cheap ticket to Bulgaria through Romania. As supposed stowaways on their deportation trip across a hostile border, we were instantly given street credibility as well as celebrity status.

The bus pulled past the guards and the guns, and once-silent passengers were now laughing in amazement at our audacity. Our new friend began to speak to us, mostly using *Scarface* and *Godfather* quotes.

"Take," he offered us some of his newly mixed protein shake. "Make you big and tough." Between swigs, he and some others passed us some Bulgarian porn magazines, I guess because all real men read porn on public buses. One guy displayed nude pictures of his girlfriend, telling us we should come to his place on the Black Sea where there would be more women just like her. They thought we were brazen and strong, like Clint Eastwood or John Wayne, possessing the same fictional American personalities as the characters in their favorite Hollywood movies.

As we disembarked in the early morning onto the gold brick streets of Sofia, some of the ex-cons gave us their addresses, asking us to visit and keep in touch. Many wanted to come to America themselves. They were very polite and friendly. Perhaps if they had spent their time in the cafés of Prague rather than in its dark alleyways they would still be there, giving their best Al Pacino impressions to other young American hopefuls.

TARA KOLDEN HAS RAMBLED AROUND
EUROPE BOTH AS A TOURIST AND FULL-
TIME RESIDENT IN GREECE, SCOTLAND,
FINLAND AND GERMANY. WHEN BACK
IN HER NATIVE SEATTLE, SHE WORKS
AS A WRITER AND FREELANCE EDITOR.

SLEEPING WITH HERCULES

TARA KOLDEN

It was late February when my friend Katy and I decided to take a weekend getaway from Athens to the Greek island of Corfu, where we spent a relaxing Saturday soaking up sunshine in the relatively deserted streets of Kerkyra, the island's main city. We ate generous helpings of *bougatsa* – a sweet concoction of milk pudding, phyllo pastry and cinnamon – and watched the sun rise over the sea without too much thought of our university courses back in Athens. Our trip had been spur-of-the-moment, executed in typical student style: no luggage, no worries, and no reservations.

We needed to be back in Athens for class on the following Tuesday, so we decided to take a Sunday-night bus out of Corfu that would take us as far as Patras. We could spend a night there and then catch a midday bus back to Athens. We knew nothing about Patras, but assumed we would find someplace to stay. We were scheduled to arrive after midnight, and I imagined slipping quietly into the darkened city and drifting toward anything with a light on. Somewhere in the back of my mind lay a small, nagging fear that nothing would be open.

I needn't have worried. It was 2 a.m. on Monday morning when we reached Patras, and *everything* was wide open. The streets were ablaze with lights, and the sidewalks crowded with hordes of revelers wearing outlandish costumes and sporting elaborately painted faces. Katy and I hailed a taxi at

CORFU

the dock and peered out its windows like first-time visitors to a strange planet as we made our way slowly through the town. I spotted a couple dressed as Doric columns. Katy pointed out a trio of jesters wearing striped outfits and tall hats accented with bells. When we asked the taxi driver if he could recommend an inexpensive place to bed down, we learned that this was the biggest carnival celebration in the Mediterranean, and every hotel in the city was booked.

Though the taxi driver was skeptical, he said he would take us to a small hotel we could try. It was deserted, but for one lone man perched on a stool at the front desk. We urgently explained our situation, but unfortunately learned that the taxi driver's skepticism was warranted: the hotel was full.

"Please," said Katy. "There's nowhere else."

The man looked at us thoughtfully for a moment. "There is a room. But only one bed."

Katy and I shrugged. "That's okay."

"Really, you don't want the room."

We insisted we did. He sighed, hoisted himself off his stool, and fished a ring of keys from his pocket. We followed him obediently down the hall, our victory tempered by the nagging feeling that there might in fact be a very good reason for us not to want the room. Would we be sharing quarters with some mythological monster – Scylla or Cerberus? Or sleeping beneath an all-night *bouzouki* band competition?

Unlocking the last door in the corridor, the proprietor reached inside, ostensibly to turn on the light. The switch made an audible click, but the only result was an almost imperceptible change in the room's luminosity. "That's it?" I thought. "Just a broken light?"

He stuck his arm into the darkened room again, with an air of mystery that made me suspect he'd reappear holding a white rabbit. Instead he withdrew five balloons, the helium-filled foil variety. For a moment I thought he was offering them to us, but then he grimaced, shook the strings in his fist, and let them drift back into the void.

"So? You take the room?"

"Sure," said Katy.

The man dropped the keys into her hand. "Keep the door closed. I give you discount," he said, and sauntered back toward the front desk. We exchanged puzzled looks, then felt our way into the darkness that now belonged to us.

When we stepped inside, indiscernible shapes jostled in every direction, and when I reached out to touch them, they bobbed away. I flinched involuntarily when something long and snakelike brushed against my face, one of countless tendrils that descended from above. Slowly attempting to straighten to my full height, my head made contact with a soft, almost ethereal ceiling that undulated and rustled. Like Amazonian interlopers, Katy and I swam through the dark shapes, causing a shift in the collective mass. For a brief moment, a tiny light shone above our heads. The bulb wasn't burned out after all – it was obscured. Before it was covered once again, I saw that Katy and I were surrounded by a jungle of balloons. Dolphins, Tweety Birds and half a dozen large, grinning incarnations of Disney's cartoon Hercules drifted in and out of view, along with a herd of dalmatians and a pair of Tasmanian devils.

Behind me, Katy was little more than a shadow. It was impossible to walk, so I dropped onto all fours and crawled through the undulating strings until my head made unexpected contact with something hard.

"The bed's over here!"

We gazed at the sea of multicolored foil faces. "Do you think they're flammable?" I didn't know for sure, but wondered at the possibility of an explosion, or suffocation.

Crawling to opposite ends of the bed, we deposited our backpacks and then struggled into pajamas in the semidarkness. It seemed almost pointless to turn out the light.

Katy suggested we try to photograph each other with the balloons. Illuminated by the flash was a large congregation of dalmatians directly above the bed, and in their midst, Hercules' unmistakable smile. He made an odd bedfellow, indistinguishable from the other shapes in the dark, but I knew he was up there, leering down at us throughout the night.

We awoke early the next morning, safely enclosed in our helium-filled cocoon. As promised, the proprietor gave us a small discount when we checked out, but what I was really hoping for was a balloon.

CHAPTER 3

GETTING IT ON

JackStraw
(3 replies)

Has this ever happened to you?

While doing a RTW trip I met what I thought was an incredible English girl (I'm American). We talked about getting married and all that. In the year and a half since we first met we've made several trips across the Atlantic to see each other. We have also had many nasty fights, both in person and over long-distance calls. We've finally called it quits after all this time, me with a plane ticket leaving to see her in London the next day, her sitting alone in an apart-ment in London that she only got in anticipation of me coming over. This is the second time this has hap-pened to me – had the same experience with a French girl about twelve years ago. Has this ever happened to anyone else? Is it not love, but rather just an intense infatuation due to meeting up while traveling in an exotic location while on holiday?

free2travel
1.

Roma Woman

I went to Rome to work for my firm and went a week early to get adjusted. The second day I was there I met a wonderful woman. Over a span of two months we had such a great time. I thought I had it all: we danced, laughed and had great sex. I was in heaven. Then I had to return to the States. I knew this girl was someone special to me so I started taking a long (four-day) weekend trip every month to see her in Rome. After having done this long-weekend trip for about five months, things just started to fall apart. The basic problem was that I couldn't move to Rome and she owned her own business and didn't want to move to the States (not that I blame her, I was born here) and we both realized that we couldn't always be on vacation. It happens to a lot of us. My suggestion:

175%   Page:

enjoy the time and unless there is a way for both of you to be on vacation all the time or to live in the same city, it is NOT going to work.

PS I have lots of frequent flyer miles now!

---

voicers
2.

You're not alone

I just returned from Europe, where I spent three months living with a lovely Italian man. For a while, it was fantastic, even though we didn't speak the same language. However, as I learned to speak Italian and to really see what life in a small Italian city is really like, the differences between us became pretty glaring and I had to tell him that I would not be returning after I left. (We'd talked about my coming back for Christmas.) We're both broken-hearted, and the cultural and language dif-ferences make it all the more difficult. I'm glad to see that I'm not the only one who lost my heart while traveling.

BpGuru
3.

Nothing new

It has been said before and will no doubt be said again: long-distance relationships rarely work out over time. Often I think it is because people confuse romance and infatuation with love. Maybe it is because our repressive English-speaking cultures tell us that deciding to just have a fling and enjoy it while it lasts is wrong. So we fool ourselves that it is love and will go on when in fact it was never going to work.

In Greece, it is normal for men of all ages to meet and romance women on holiday for a week or two.

There is a name for a man who does this: *Kamaki*.
Loosely translated it means a fisherman who fishes
for women. It is considered quite honorable and the
older men will sit in the *taverna* and talk about how in
their day they were real *kamikis* who offered a woman
romance and love for as long as it lasted, while the
younger men of today are just after the sex and don't
really care for the woman, etc. The movie *Shirley
Valentine* was very true to life. Kiss her goodbye and
vow eternal love, then head to the bar to meet the
next one.

My point is that holiday or travel romances should be
accepted for what they are: temporary. If you go into
a relationship knowing that, there is very little hurt
when it ends as expected.

LISA K. BUCHANAN'S AWARD-WINNING
FICTION AND ESSAYS HAVE APPEARED
IN *COSMOPOLITAN, REDBOOK,
CALIFORNIA LAWYER* AND IN MAGAZINES
PUBLISHED IN IRELAND, SOUTH
AFRICA, CANADA AND JAPAN. HER
MASTER OF FINE ARTS IS FROM MILLS
COLLEGE. LISA IS BASED IN SAN
FRANCISCO AND ENJOYS TRAVELING
TO OTHER WALKABLE CITIES.

FORTRESS

LISA K. BUCHANAN

Kostas pressed the last bite of baklava and two honey-soaked fingers into my mouth. I took the pastry and returned the fingers, dangling my legs over the thick stone wall of the Corfu fortress.

"Corfu is fighting invasion for centuries," he said. "The Venetians, the Turks, the French, the Russians, the Italians, the Germans. But the Turks, they are the worst. They conquer all of Greece, but not Corfu. This fortress save us; save Corfu from the Turks."

"Why all the invasions?" I asked, with the innocence of one whose home-soil had, at the time, not been attacked since Pearl Harbor.

Kostas rolled his eyes and took my chin in his hand. "Corfu is the jewel and everyone wants to own her."

We struggled onward, our verbal attempts as warm and murky as the Mediterranean Sea lapping against the stone walls below us. I was twenty-five and on vacation, open, rootless, blithely remiss on names I had memorized without zeal – Bunker Hill, the Boston Tea Party, the Bill of Rights. But Kostas wasn't concerned about the historical and geographical ignorance he had come to expect from American tourists. Nuzzling his soft, Greek beard into my cheek, he leaned into me, a tank pushing through a thicket, flattening my fingers into limp blades.

CORFU

"Kostas, tell me more about the fortress."

"You are a fortress. How many centuries till I break down the wall and kiss you, my sugar candy?"

"I think you mean 'Sweetie.' And it will be ages. It was only this morning, you know, that you stood behind me at the bus depot and pretended to be reading the schedule."

"Sweetzie," he said, "you take out a cigarette because you know I am lighting it for you. You drop the tissue paper. Now we kiss."

The handkerchief, I did not reply as he grinned, slowly licking the honey from his sticky lips.

"And now, show me the rest of the fortress," I said, finding my feet, "so I can hear how Napoleon took the island."

"Bloody tourist," he grumbled, a phrase he'd learned, no doubt, from a British woman some previous summer, walking around the fortress and having her cigarettes lit for her. Leaping ahead of me, he took my hand, squeezing it just a little too hard. We hiked along the top of a thick stone wall, and occasionally he glanced back at me, pouting. I twinkled, trying not to be smug about this burly seaman who, at thirty-four, still lived at home with his parents.

"Okay, I tell you about the Venetians. In the 1300s, they occupy Corfu. They are bad to the Greek peoples, but they build this fortress. Then the Turkish Army invades, and they make slaves of everybody. That's when the Venetians bring in the cobblestone–"

Kostas stopped and faced me mid-sentence, claiming a strict hold on my hips with his square hands, pulling me close so our chins almost touched. He fired his eyes, green grenades, into mine with impeccable aim.

"Now you kiss me," he commanded. When I didn't cooperate, he glared from behind dark brows.

"A tease," he said, releasing me. "You have no passion."

"It's true. Call me in three days; we'll have lunch."

I took his hand and we walked, man and woman, each cocksure of winning over the other. I envisioned us at a small table, drinking red wine in a tavern with a boisterous bartender; I saw Kostas talking to me about weak coffee and menus in English, the rape of Corfu by Turks and tourists; I thought of him peering back at me over his shoulder after a protracted, delectable kiss outside my pensione; I saw a moonlit night of solitary, coveted longing.

But in *his* mind we were climbing the fortress to a secluded refuge to writhe on the ground, my hair secured in his victorious palm. He saw me tossing aside my mannered reserve, my prissy concept of longing, my sweatshirt and shorts. He imagined me panting into his neck, my urgent fingers on his shoulders.

Amid our separate visions, we continued climbing atop the stone wall that spiraled around the fortress.

"Kostas, what about Napoleon?"

My hairy Greek man sighed.

"Napoleon sends the army and takes us from the Venetians. Then we fight the French and Russians. Then the Turks again, then Napoleon again, and the French people build ugly houses by the Esplanade. And now, Sweetzie, time for me to have you. Why you do not kiss me?"

Accustomed to the call-me-later men at home, I was baffled by Kostas, who knew how to turn on the soup but hadn't the patience to let it simmer.

"Hey, back off," I told him when he lunged for me. "This is getting old."

"What do you mean, this back-off?"

"You know what I mean. Stop whining."

He swiped his hand from mine and folded his arms over his chest. "I do not whine you. I am want you."

"Kostas, let's turn back. It's getting dark."

"No, Sugar Candy, we climb to the top and you see all of Corfu. Beautiful night."

"I want to go back." At this, Kostas jumped down onto a ledge, where I could barely see him in the darkening dusk.

"Come," he said. "Into my arms."

But when I knelt down ready to slide, he hopped back, out of reach.

"First, you promise my kiss."

"Hey, help me down off here."

"My kiss."

"Not funny anymore, Kostas."

He paced, the top of his curly head leagues beneath my feet. Waves crashed in the distance and I weighed my possible fates: Kostas, crouched and waiting to pounce. Or me, waiting him out, landing scraped and dirty with a sprained ankle, wandering around this haunted battleground, alone but for the bitter souls of hollow-eyed soldiers. In the harbor glow, I saw his dark form leaning against a rock, eerily patient.

Kostas was mad at the Turks for their sixteenth-century invasion, and mad at me for my contemporary resistance, my American preoccupation with levity. He had brawny shoulders, calloused palms, sea-smell in his hair. He had night vision at the fortress, a maze of chambers, trenches, trails and twisted trees. Most important, he had history, the ancestral terrain, where he and his friends had played as boys, reenacting Turkish invasions, executing the enemy with finger guns, scrambling with ease over ledges such as this one.

"Kostas, how about if you help me down and we go to a tavern?"

"My kiss."

"But it's getting cold."

"I am wait for you as long as you like, Sugar Candy. If you did not want me, you would not come here with me."

"I want to go to the tavern."

"I am want you."

Could an hour have passed? His cigarette flashed orange in the dark and occasionally his shoes made a scraping noise. Gone were my fantasies of longing for him through the night. I wanted to want; he wanted to have. There seemed to be no middle ground.

The wall had become cold against my back. Straining my eyes in a futile attempt to see the ground below my feet, I wished that my panic were just a foreigner's flash and that somehow we could retrieve the simple flirtation of the afternoon. If not, I would settle for being alone in my rented room, safe and warm, behind a thick, locked door and the scrupulous watch of the German granny at the front desk. At last, he spoke.

"We go now, Sweetzie, I am hungry."

"I'm hungry too," I said. "Help me down?"

Kostas sighed. "I take you to the tavern. I help you down."

A ploy? Possibly, but I couldn't find it in myself to spurn a reprieve.

Comforted by the fatigue in his voice and the time that had passed, I slid cautiously down the wall, the seaman's hands steadying my feet, knees and thighs. He set me on the ground gently, a shop-keeper returning a glass figurine to the shelf. Hand in hand, we walked toward the town, waving our invisible white flags at each other in the dark.

BRITISH WRITER DIANA OMO EVANS
HAS WORKED EXTENSIVELY AS AN EDI-
TOR AND JOURNALIST FOR *MARIE
CLAIRE*, THE *INDEPENDENT*, *EVENING
STANDARD*, *THE SOURCE*, NME.COM,
THE STAGE, AND *PRIDE MAGAZINE*.
RECENT TRIPS HAVE TAKEN HER TO
CUBA, TANZANIA, MONTSERRAT AND
WASHINGTON STATE, WHERE SHE COM-
PLETED A WRITER'S RESIDENCY.

THE LOVE OF STRANGERS

DIANA OMO EVANS

The streets in Paris are wide open avenues of freedom or danger, depending on what time of day it is, how old you are, and whether or not you have a roof over your head. Parentless and abroad for the first time, it was dark, we were sixteen, and there was no room at the inn.

Paris was the first stop on the Evans Twins' carefully mapped month-long Euro-Tour. After we'd taken in the Eiffel Tower and the Parisian unknown, we'd nip into Munich and Cologne for a week or so, zoom across to Austria, head for the rolling green slopes and clear lakes of Switzerland and then tumble down to Italy, to drift through Venice and walk through the ruins of Rome.

On the ferry to Calais that morning, Paula and I had leaned over the railings to catch sea spray on our cheeks, chattering about The Great Adventure.

"I bet you'll have an affair," said Paula as we tasted the salt. She was already clipped to a boy called Francis, a seventeen-year-old guitar prodigy from Essex whose first gift to her had been a pair of leopard-print earmuffs that were now getting wet.

"Aren't your ears feeling soggy?" I asked, trying to change the subject. I had a reputation for being the family floozy because on our filial holidays to Corfu or Brittany or Morocco, I was always the one who ended up being snogged by some boy, usually curly-haired and unnaturally tall. I had said I love you to boys whose names I had forgotten.

PARIS

The train from Calais to Paris was long and tiring. We'd slept some of the way, still drowsy from the Channel crossing, but had woken up when a woman had sat opposite us. She was wearing a suit and looked hassled, as if she'd just come out of a really heavy meeting, or had a fight in the post office. She looked us over. Two days before our departure, we'd both done our hair in tiny plaits so we wouldn't have to bother about grappling with frizz. Paula had put red and yellow beads at the ends of hers. Gradually, the woman's eyelids began falling and it became apparent that she was a person who slept with her mouth open, like Dad, who each night filled the house with a terrible snoring. Her head lolled about on the headrest, jolted regularly by the speeding train, and we could see the back of her throat. Another jolt would wake her and she'd snap her eyes open and close her big sticky mouth, until sleep stretched it open again, her drying tongue and gums and tooth fillings laid out for inspection.

"Quick, where's the camera?" Paula giggled. I was rummaging around in my bag and we were both laughing as silently as we could, but again the woman woke up. We'd almost had her.

We turned our attention to the flying landscape at the window, bright summer fields on a clear blue horizon. I slept again and dreamt of a little girl in a pleated dress standing by the tracks with quick green trees behind her, watching our train go by.

Paris was full. Paula and I looked like turtles with long legs as we trekked from hostel to hostel trying to beat dusk. To find ourselves shelterless on the first night of our adventure would be disastrous.

The last place we tried was on a dusty backstreet. It was already dark when we got there, and we could see the silhouettes of men hanging around under the streetlight outside the hostel. We'd ridden the metro three times that afternoon, swooning under our backpacks as people shoved past us, and were desperate.

"I'd sleep anywhere," I puffed as we trod heavily through the glass double doors. The place was bare and brightly lit. A group of kids were sitting on the floor next to their bags, looking fed up. They watched us hopelessly as we waddled up to the counter.

It is always difficult to remember the initial, unknown face of a person you come to know, to erase from it the stories you later discover, or guess. Soft, flickering eyes, he had, and wisps of black hair touching them, a slightly nerdy smile, long beige teeth. His name was Ben, and he seemed genuinely disappointed to have to break the news that there were no rooms available. Paula sank against the counter.

"What, nothing? Nothing at all? We have to stay *somewhere*," I begged. The group on the floor gave us sympathetic looks. Ben told us they were waiting to see if there were any cancellations, "or sudden vacations – like if someone gets sick and has to be rushed to hospital immediately, or even dies. You never know what's going to crop up," he said, in an accent drifting between America, France and Scotland. His hyperactive eyes skipped across my face. "Have a seat – I'll see what I can do."

We planted ourselves on our backpacks and waited. No one died or suddenly took ill. "What are we going to do?" I asked Paula. She was leant forward on her knees, using her arms as a pillow.

"We'll stay here," she mumbled through her sleeve. Paula could sleep anywhere, on cue. I was used to hearing her, breathing deeply across the room within five minutes of lying down, while I still waited for sleep to come for me. The kids on the floor got up wearily and started lifting their bags. The oldest was a chubby boy of about eighteen in dirty jeans and a vest. He picked up another bag and walked out into the night, his companions dragging after him.

I was beginning to accept Paula's conclusion. She had already slid onto me, and begun to doze, when Ben leaned over the counter.

"Hey, sorry, loves, but there's nothing. Hostel rule is no sleeping in the lobby and the only other option is my room."

"Really?" I said.

"Sure. I've got a spare mattress. It'll be fine for a night, then you can find somewhere tomorrow."

Paula woke up and eyed him. Besides a slight coyness, he radiated innocence and romantic disinterest. We silently decided it was better than a strange street on a black night in a new country.

"Okay then," I said, and Paula thanked him sweetly. He just had to lock up, he told us, and then he'd be all ours.

"Just the room will be fine, thanks," muttered Paula when he disappeared again.

His room was littered with piles of clothing, bags and books. Jars with nothing in them, bars of soap still in their wrappers, socks in balls, pens and dust. There was one table, with a tub of salt, an ashtray and some notebooks on it. Ben told us he'd worked for a company in Scotland that sold cigarettes before going traveling. He'd been to Japan, California, Brazil and Turkey. Paris ran him dry and he was stuck here until he could save enough money to move on. Where were we headed? I explained the route we'd planned while he dragged a mattress into the center of the room, then another, and pushed them together.

"It's okay," Paula said quickly, "we can share."

"Oh, don't worry." Ben spread out a couple of faded sheets and dropped pillows on top of them. "You'll be comfier this way." Then he pressed his lips together and opened them again, as if he was suppressing a thought. "What do you think I'm going to do, anyway?"

Paula's face darkened. She went next door to the bathroom with her bag of toiletries and some clothes to sleep in. Ben leaned against the desk with his leg propped up on the chair next to it, and I noticed something both seductive and sinister. He looked at me as if he couldn't help it, as if convinced I wanted him to. It fabricated a vague desire in me, the want that comes from being wanted, but quickly fades when you get it.

When Paula came back in she lay down on the farthest side of the bed. That meant I had the groove in the middle.

Ben put on a tape of Billie Holiday's "God Bless the Child," and said that his mother got him into Billie and he liked her heartbreak. "Tragedy makes things interesting. I mean, it makes you learn big things and offers the achievement of overcoming. Don't you think?"

"Not tragedy," I said, though he was a decade older than me and probably knew better, "but struggle. People don't always get over tragedies."

I wondered what he'd been through as I got into bed. In the faint glow of the lamp I saw him undress. He was skinny, all lank and gangle with unfortunate knees. He left his boxers on and got in next to me. I thought it seemed a little ungracious to be so bare in bed with strangers, making it virtually impossible for us, in the liberty and forgetfulness of sleep, not to encounter the private heat of his skin.

I dreamt I was on a lake, gliding across it in a rowing boat. A woman was with us, wet hair and breasts browning in the sun, behind her the lilac mountains. And on the other side of the lake, where we were headed, someone was watching us and waiting. Then I felt the brush of him on my back. He took me away from the water and back into his dark, foreign sheets. It took me a moment to place myself. Lying behind me, his hand began moving across my stomach, beneath my clothes, softly, slowly, secretly. Up to where my breasts began, over the curve there, upwards to my shoulder. There is some art in touching, achieving the right balance of tenderness and intent. I lay still, feigning sleep, outraged yet enjoying the hand roaming me, as if it was not connected to anyone. When he tried to slip between my legs I pressed them together and stopped him.

In the morning the walls were white and the ceiling high, sunshine falling in from the window. Paula had risen early as usual, and when I opened my eyes she was leaning out of the window. Ben was gone. Paula told me he'd said we could leave our things there while we looked for another place. I told her about the night's activities. She was shocked, but I more so: those same hands had reached across me to fondle her shoulder and back before she'd woken up and shuffled away in disgust. "The pervert," she said. "The bloody pervert."

Yet we stayed there another night. And three weeks later, we stopped off in Paris to see him on our way to Switzerland. The words came to me from nowhere, perhaps because he was my Euro-Tour lover and there had been times I'd missed the idea of him, or perhaps because he had told me once as Billie moaned in the background that he worshipped me.

Into his ear, miserably, I whispered, "I love you."

CAROL SCHWALBERG IS THE WIDELY
TRAVELED AUTHOR OF TWO CHILDREN'S
BOOKS AND A COLLECTION OF SATIR-
ICAL ESSAYS.

A FINE ITALIAN HAND

CAROL SCHWALBERG

I snuck past a group of them dawdling over ice cream at a table
fronting the sidewalk. "*Bella, bella,*" they called. Sinking into a seat
at the rear of the café, I had hardly ordered coffee and unfolded the
International Herald Tribune when a guy at the next table spoke up.

"*Signorina*, you are American?"

"How did you know?"

"Your dress. Many American women choose this mode." I was
wearing a tank top. Fashion taken care of, he confided that with my
dark hair and eyes, I appeared Italian.

"My mother was born in Naples," I confessed.

The lie appeared to please him, as he nodded and gestured
toward the newspaper. "Your president, he will win the election for
parliament?"

He must have meant the congressional election. "I don't know.
I'm suffering from an advanced case of museum feet, and I was
about to read the comics." I held them up.

He smiled. "You are . . . you are –" His well of English had
run dry. "*Molto allegre e bella.*"

The usual blather. It was funny, though, how Italian men
upgraded from attractive to ravishing. Besides, he was handsome enough, and reading a book of poetry. But too young,
like half of the ones who ever said anything. The other half
were married.

ITALY

I smiled, which released a name – Onofrio Campanella – and another barrage of Italian compliments.

At the front table, other young men were shouting at women walking by, and no one under sixty escaped their remarks. One young girl shot them a sneer, and they responded in turn with insult.

Our conversation wound on, and I told him about my home, my travel plans, and what I thought of Italy, wondering in the back of my mind what his mother would think of him wooing a Jewish American divorcée.

Suddenly he glanced at his watch and slapped his forehead. "*Accidenti!*"

"What's the matter?"

Dropping coins onto the table, he leapt out of his chair. "I shall be late! The train waits not!"

"You spent half an hour chatting me up! After all of this," I asked, "you're going to leave?"

Onofrio smiled. "It is never a waste of time to make friends with a *bella*." He turned and bolted toward the railway station.

Watching his receding behind, I realized how it worked: Italian men pick up women the way tennis players practice their backhand. To improve their performance.

DAVID-MATTHEW BARNES' FICTION,
POETRY AND STAGE PLAYS HAVE
APPEARED IN SEVERAL LITERARY
JOURNALS AND MAGAZINES. HE WROTE
AND DIRECTED THE INDEPENDENT
TEEN FILM, *FROZEN STARS*.

AND I LOVED A SOLDIER

DAVID-MATTHEW BARNES

After working for seven months and twelve days at a snack bar in a bowling alley in Sacramento, I saved everything that had been given to me via a tip jar on an orange-painted counter. I was nineteen, and each night after work, I would count out the crumpled bills and greasy bits of change, all of it inching me closer to the world, my determination fierce and wicked. In June, I went to a frizzy-haired travel agent with a huge overbite and cheap airplane tickets. Handing her a handful of green and silver, she gave me my freedom. I left the next morning.

After I saw a woman shoot heroin into her arm in a back alley in Amsterdam, I boarded a train at Centraal Station and left the canals and drugs behind. In Munich I ate pastries, honey nut and cherry, shared carrots with a German girl named Sandra, held babies from Belgrade. I saw Europe through the window of a train bound for the Mediterranean. And that was when I met you, a man from Kossovo Polje. Hair dark like my past. Eyes shimmering with purity, cheekbones reaching heartbreaking heights.

You were the soldier who bought me a Coke and drank me up. Standing side by side in the bar, the connection was immediate and caused my spine to tighten. In broken English, you announced that you would make my journey your own, postponing your trip home, and hoping to find the same sense of comfort with me.

GREECE

In Athens, we slept in a bed for the first time in a week on the third floor of the Hotel Olympus. With the French doors open, we inhaled the smells of Omonia Square, dreamt of soldiers and babies, Belgrade and war, the sunny concave of California shores. In the morning we drank orange Fantas, changed my Lincolns for drachmas, and caught a subway to Piraeus to board a ship called the *Aegean*. My legs and feet were sunburned, and we careened around the Cyclades, looking for Homer and an island called Ios, where you promised we'd fall in love.

We drank piña coladas at the Cava Doro, stumbled down donkey trails and discovered passion on the sands of Milopotas Beach. You told me you had never known life to be so sweet. I told you of the bitterness I left behind which led me to Europe, which led me to you.

Twelve days later, we realized I had no more American money. We had to find work. And so I became a dancer at Scorpions, standing on an elevated circle while the DJ made sexual advances. But he always played my favorite song, and the cigarette girl slipped me packs of Marlboros on a regular basis.

We moved to a new campground where clothes were washed with rocks, where women gutted fish in the kitchen, sometimes with their bare hands. To make us more money, I cleaned bathrooms three times a day. You built houses of wire and straw with the hands that held my own when I became frightened of the future. Sometimes when I'd cross the campground, I'd catch your eye, and you'd watch me balance my orange and black skulled bucket of poison against my hip, as if I were cradling our fate against my body.

Then we were separated by the Gulf War, and fear, like fatigue, cast over our existence. Americans were evacuated, and I was rushed, forced to shove my things into a backpack. I searched for you in the faces of the crowd, as helicopters landed and took off again like confused pelicans. I screamed your name while being shoved in with the other frightened Americans. At lift-off, I saw you running to me, and for the first time in my life, contemplated jumping.

The edge of our inevitable goodbye has already frayed, yet stands before me, looming. I will constantly grope in a stranger's darkness, permanently frustrated, comparing all others to what I once had, if only fleetingly.

MO FLEMING IS A FOLK ARTIST WHOSE
LAP QUILTS HAVE BEEN EXHIBITED IN
NEW YORK AND NEW JERSEY. SHE IS
CURRENTLY WORKING ON A NON-
FICTION BOOK ABOUT BLACK WOMEN
AND JUDAISM.

FRENCH SPEAKEASY

MO FLEMING

The walk-up café was at the edge of pedestrian hell, a story above rue St.-Something-or-Other and Boulevard Who-the-Hell-Remembers, with a splendid view of light-winking "gay Paree." French drivers rushed to mayhem in those ugly old Citroëns that looked like Volkswagen Beetles on heroin. Pedestrians barely avoided massive body trauma as they raced from one side of the road to the other. I thought I was safe inside.

I loved my brief Parisian sojourn: the cheesy pensione with the slender window of opportunity for a hot morning shower, my funky bidet, the musty smell of my room under the roof.

Although I barely understood a word of it, the French language was my ideal clitoral stimulant. I would have traded my lusty lingerie for a paragraph *parlezed* into my ear, even though every man I had met so far smoked like the volcanoes that eventually buried Montserrat.

"Jacques" sat at the table next to mine, and was, naturally, smoking, the pack of Gitanes lounging beside his *demitasse*. There was nothing "Hollywood French" about him, no beret, no Marcel Marceau striped shirt, none of the burly peasant exuded by Gérard Depardieu. But he at least sounded like the debonair actor Charles Boyer when he spoke.

"*Et vous Afrique?*"

Intrigued, I tried to take in his affirmative particulars. He had enough hair on his hands and arms to blush the average

PARIS

105

mandrill malachite with envy. His eyes were slate gray, and he wore a look of Indochine war and innocence unrecoverable. This didn't make him handsome. His most distinguishing feature was the careless growth of stubble that oh so subtly suggested that he didn't give a damn about shaving.

Afrique I understood. I sipped my espresso, wishing I actually liked strong bitter java, and attempted a jaded facade of sophistication, sex, and *je ne sais quoi*, even though I wanted to retch le café on le table.

"*Je suis Americaine*," I said nonchalantly. I was trying to sound like a) I sat around cafés speaking French every day, and b) he was lucky I was letting him talk to me at all.

His eyes said, "Ah," but his lips repeated after mine, "*Americaine*." Only he said it with a heat that burned like the sands of Algerique. And he said it a breath away from my earlobe, because "Jacques" had palmed his pack of cigarettes, taken a big, final slurp from his tiny cup, and had relocated (uninvited) to sit wrist distant from my left nipple. He lit another cigarette, leaned in close, and began to rap in la lingua de la sticky lingerie.

What's the French word for easy? *Facile*? *Je suis facile. Je suis* shamelessly easy *Afrique Amerique*.

SINCE HIS EUROPEAN SUMMER GAVE
RYAN THE TRAVEL BUG, HE HAS TRAV-
ELED AROUND THE WORLD ABOARD A
SHIP, EARNED A TEACHING CERTIFI-
CATE IN THAILAND, HONEYMOONED IN
TANZANIA, WORKED AT A YOUTH HOSTEL
NEAR SAN FRANCISCO, AND VOLUN-
TEERED WITH A TURTLE PROTECTION
PROGRAM IN MEXICO. RYAN LIVES IN
OBERLIN, OHIO, WITH HIS WIFE KACI.

THE LITTLE MOTHER

RYAN FORSYTHE

Wilhelm Raabe, a German writer, once exclaimed, "Oh, Prague, what a piece of my free soul you took away from me!" After spending six days strolling through the mystical capital of the Czech Republic, Prague took more than just my soul. It took my Kathy.

A month before the big trip, I broke up with my girlfriend, then bought a plane ticket and a brand-new backpack. Dad had pulled all the suitcases out of the attic for me to look over, but I told him I wanted to travel a bit lighter, to step off the plane with nothing but the bag upon my back.

I figured I'd first secure a room for the night. After validating my Eurailpass at the airport, my train adventure began as I made my way to the Frankfurt Haus der Jugend. There my first hosteling experience began with a hot shower followed by a not-so-hot meal of meatloaf, scalloped potatoes, green beans and a Coke.

Later that night, I found myself down in the lobby, playing cards and sharing dumb jokes with a guy named Blaine from California. It became a contest, which of us had the worst riddle. Most were groaners, at least that was the response elicited from the young lady in the corner thumbing through a fashion magazine.

"Want to join us?" Blaine asked.

"No," she said. "I'm waiting for a friend."

PRAGUE

We continued with the jokes, but could hear her chuckling behind her magazine. I thought we should try again.

"Mind if we join you?"

"I guess that'd be cool. What're you guys playing?"

Just then her friend showed up. "Euchre," I answered. "Now we have four."

Kathy and Molly were about two weeks into their own two-month trek around Europe. In the morning they would be making their way to Berlin, Munich or Prague, they informed me, and asked if I wanted to join them.

I was a bit split on this. A third of me wanted to go with them, a third wanted to stay and check out Frankfurt, and a third didn't want to impose. Since that was two-thirds against, I declined. After a few rounds of cards, stories, and the obligatory tips for touring this crazy old continent, they wished me the best of luck and realized I hadn't told them my name.

"Just call me Mr. Man," I winked. With that, Kathy and Molly were gone.

I soon found that Frankfurt was not the greatest city for just hanging around. It seemed industrial, like Detroit. So within two days, I was on to Munich. The information booth at the train station provided maps for a few youth hostels, and I picked one at random. Fortunately my train arrived early enough for me to get to the Jugendherberge before it opened for check-in.

I pulled out my card deck while waiting in the hostel lobby, and the one trick I knew was enough to impress the Japanese people who arrived just after me. After an hour of chatting with strangers, I heard a familiar voice.

"Hey! It's Mr. Man."

Kathy and Molly were back! They had spent the last few nights in this very hostel and were heading out to Dachau. We made plans to have dinner.

The heart of Germany has a strong Turkish population, so we decided to test our tongues on this cuisine, as sausages, potatoes and beer were growing old. After dinner we went to a beer garden and that is where it happened. That's when I fell in love with Kathy.

It was the night before the fourth of July, I remember, because we were the only ones celebrating. Kicking back a couple of steins of dark beer, we passed the hours trading life experiences.

I have always been known as a storyteller among my friends – perhaps a little too well known. As soon as I begin any of my tales, they either run from the room, or rush to cover my mouth. Not Kathy, though.

"Your turn, Mr. Man," she said, after talking about how she and Molly had met at age five. "Make it a good one."

"I guess I could tell you about the time I met Kim Deal," I began.

"Kim Deal?" Kathy interrupted.

"Yeah, she was the bassist for the Pixies and is now lead singer of the Breeders."

"I know who Kim Deal is – I love her!" she exclaimed. "You actually met her?"

Kathy was the only person who listened attentively throughout, asking relevant questions, and *oohing* and *ahhing* at appropriate moments. What was formerly the ten-minute Kim Deal Story became the two-hour Kim Deal Experience as I included every little detail I could remember from the three minutes I shared with my rock star hero. And after my tale had ended, the three of us discussed our favorite parts of the story, I repeated a few of them, and then we all joined in singing our favorite Pixies and Breeders songs.

The fact that Kathy could completely delight in my own experience, that she truly understood the power and meaning of it, told me something about her. We would forever be connected.

Molly then noted it was 12:45 and the hostel locked its gates at precisely one in the morning (apparently, they had tested this the night before). Jumping up, we ran to the nearest bus stop, and arrived back just in time, as the manager was unlocking his padlock to clamp onto the iron gate.

Just before they reached their room, Kathy informed me that they would be heading to Berlin the next day. Though I wanted to stay on in Munich and see some of the sites, I wasn't prepared to lose Kathy again. The odds were probably against my randomly running into her a third time. I asked her to take me with them.

"We'll talk," Kathy replied. "Breakfast. Seven-thirty."

I often wonder what Kathy and Molly said to each other after retiring to their room, the individual opinions about the guy they had just met on their European vacation. Was I just tagging along?

At least one of them seemed to have no problem with it. The next morning, as soon as we sat down to our continental breakfasts, it was understood that we were going to be traveling together.

I stayed with Kathy and Molly for the next ten days.

Franz Kafka was right when he wrote, "Prague doesn't release you. This *Mutterchen* (little mother) has claws." Though we had planned on staying only two days there, Kathy and Molly remained for almost a week, and it took me even longer to escape.

I wasn't sure how it happened, but as soon as we arrived, Prague felt like home. Traveling through a foreign continent, visiting a different city every few days, often discovering a different language each time, it is difficult to feel truly comfortable in any one locale. Yet stepping off the train in Prague, I knew I had found something special.

Prague is cordial, warmhearted. After an hour, it is a familiar friend. Hradèany Castle dominates the skyline, as it has done for the past thousand years, and everywhere you turn, from Wenceslas Square to the banks of the Vltava River and the former Prague Ghetto, you feel a connection to this so-called City of a Hundred Spires.

Each night, we dined in style, whether it was roast pork with dumplings and sauerkraut at U Radnice, nachos and beer at Jo's Bar, or just crepes at a street stand. Then we would stroll across Charles Bridge, tossing coins to the street performers who danced with their marionettes.

Kathy and Molly were getting restless, however. It wasn't that they didn't love staring at the statue of Saint Wenceslas in Nové Mesto, or waiting for Death to ring its knell on the astronomical clock in the Staré Mesto. They had a rough itinerary of places to discover before heading back home, and they wanted to stick to it.

Finally, they announced a plan to head to Hungary on the night train. I really wanted to go with them, I still had to profess my love to Kathy, after all. But one thing kept me from going with them: Prague. To stay less than one week seemed immoral.

And so, torn two ways, I regretfully ended my sojourn for the moment with Kathy and Molly. We made plans to meet eight days later in Athens, at 2:45 on a Saturday afternoon.

That night, I saw them off at the train station. Standing on the platform, I looked up at them, as the train started to hum. Kathy asked if I had any more gum, so I took the one piece in my pocket and handed it up through the window. Just as the train started to pull out of the station, she took it, split it, and handed me back a third. "Three ways," she smiled. "Friends forever." And with that she was gone.

I never saw Kathy or Molly again. They didn't show up at our meeting spot in Athens that Saturday, Sunday, or Monday either. I guess Prague didn't take Kathy away from me. Rather, the city kept me from her.

LISA GUEST IS A LICENSED MASSEUSE TO THE STARS. SHE IS CURRENTLY WORKING ON A BOOK CHRONICLING ON-LINE DATING.

SAILING
LISA GUEST

"Sailing" by Christopher Cross came out the summer I traveled to Europe at the age of twenty. Halfway through my Berkeley undergraduate education, I was experiencing a mind and body meltdown, and needed time off. Instead of a semester to think for myself, I had only the summer and a backpack with which to explore.

I spent nine idyllic days on Mykonos making friends with the natives. Their day job was to transport tourists on their fishing boats from Platys Gialos to the island's three separate and distinct southern beaches: Paradise (mellow mainstream), Super Paradise (quite nude), and Elia (blatantly gay). I spent most of those nine days on the boats sailing from beach to beach, smelling suntan lotion and souvlaki, watching bikini-clad and completely bare hedonists find their spot on the sand or up at the bar where the beer was cheap and cold. Day after day, I was a treasured guest on ancient boats that had been handed down from one male member of the family to the next.

I loved the back and forth motion, dropping people off, picking people up, moving them to another beach. My hands and feet drifted along in the cold ocean rhythm. I found peace in the long hot hours in the sun, feeling the stiffness of salt water dried onto my arms and legs, zoning out amidst the many mingled foreign voices I couldn't understand and didn't need to comprehend. I dropped my Type-A personal-

GREECE

112

ity overboard, and, for the first time in my life, learned about relaxation.

As unwound as I'd ever been, I began to develop something for Georgos, one of the captains. In his early forties, with a macho gruffness, he was like the king of the island. His face was weathered, his teeth not all present under a thick long moustache, but his entire body was like a moving sculpture of milk chocolate. Every day I'd quietly watch him entertain his passengers: standing on one hand, dancing around the boat, pulling all sizes and shapes of people onto his lap, nonchalantly steering the boat with his bare foot on the tiller. Male and female tourists alike favored him as their captain, and waited until they could get a ride on his boat. After just a few days, I too could be found only on this aging Adonis of a man's stern.

By the end of the trip, when he cooked octopus and crab and kept filling my glass with ouzo, I slipped into bed with him. Like the sea urchins he caught and shucked for lunch one day, he was prickly on the outside, but raw and vulnerable when alone in his home. The next morning it seemed as if the whole island knew that Georgos had found his woman. He asked me to stay, but I left the island two days later, pushing myself forward into uncertainty.

When I returned home, "Sailing" was a big hit. Every time I heard it, I was transported back onto the boat with its peeling paint and primitive man.

GINU KAMANI HAS BEEN ASKED WHETHER
SHE IS FROM AFGHANISTAN, BENGAL,
BOLIVIA, BRAZIL, CHILE, ECUADOR,
EGYPT, ETHIOPIA, FIJI, GOA,
GUJARAT, GUYANA, HAWAII, IRAN,
ISRAEL, KERALA, MAHARASHTRA,
MAURITIUS, MEXICO, PAKISTAN,
PERU, PUERTO RICO, PUNJAB, SPAIN,
TRINIDAD, TURKEY AND VENEZUELA.
SHE LIVES IN NORTHERN CALIFORNIA.

EPIPHANY

GINU KAMANI

My first encounter with Greek food changed my life. I was twenty-five years old, traveling through Europe on my way to India and was glad to finally be in Greece, meeting up with "K," a friend from my graduate program. K and Pop, her father, collected me from the Hania airport on Crete. She was five feet tall, as was he. His enormous belly swung before him.

We set out for the beach house. Like many Greeks, Pop drove in darkness with the headlights off. This supposedly helped save on the car battery, but basically provided cheap thrills. Some ouzo kept me detached, and my cultural exposure to reincarnation came in handy as we hurtled along the winding road. Finally we passed the last village before descending to the beach house. My friend shouted greetings of reassurance up and down the road, receiving slightly hostile rumbles of recognition in exchange.

I awoke the next morning to the smell of coffee. The thick brew was served unfiltered in small cups, accompanied by fruit, bread, butter, honey and *mizithra*, a wonderfully tangy cheese. My experience of cheese until then had been limited to cheddar, cream cheese and Swiss. Following instructions, I layered honey and *mizithra* on thick chunks of bread, a previously incomprehensible combination for me. It was delicious. The family procured a variety of other cheeses: sharp, nutty

GREECE

114

ghravyera and *kefalotiri*, the standard feta and also sheep's milk yogurt, as thick and pungent as cheese.

The charm of any beach house is, of course, eating fresh seafood. Every afternoon Pop met with returning fishermen. He brought back thick purple octopus, monkfish and lobster that resembled armored tanks. The seafood was grilled, sautéed, steamed or poached. No breading or deep frying. This first immersion into the essence of fish reminded me ecstatically of certain amorous encounters with humans.

An appetite for internal organs was strongly evident in this family, and everyone cleaned out their fish heads except me. Determining that I had indeed rejected my portion, K grabbed the head and sucked it dry. Similarly, every spindly leg of the lobster was lovingly cracked and consumed.

I surrendered my unwanted rejects, content to sip my red wine. This household cultivated grapes and pressed their own wine, adding to a vat that included distillations ten years old. Until now, American jug wines had defined the extent of my experience. This wine was exquisite: ruby red, dense, fruity, full-bodied. Pop warned me that it was rationed so I had to make do with one glass a day. Unrationed spirits included retsina and ouzo. I had no complaints.

Unbeknownst to me, K had a reputation as a woman with balls, and so, long before the main meal, she and I were each presented with a single sphere of dark meat. She popped this item nonchalantly into her mouth. "What is it?" I asked, probing with my fork.

"Eat!" barked Pop, who watched me chew then held up his ouzo in salute. Kidney? Liver? My friend revealed the mystery meat as a cock's testicle. I looked up with a start, causing the men to laugh appreciatively and regard me with renewed interest.

Locals stopped by the house after lunch, inviting us to join them in diving for sea urchin roe. My friend jumped at the chance, and I accompanied her. Sea urchin roe are considered on par with caviar, and I had tasted neither. We traveled to a beautiful bay with crystal clear water. The divers needed unmuddied shallows to escape being punctured by the sea urchin spines. The operation of locating pregnant specimens was entirely hit-and-miss. But once the egg-loaded spheres were split open, they revealed their bounty in orange-red veins. By sunset, the treasure amounted to three tablespoons worth of roe. Around us were littered the remains of dozens of spiny creatures. The precious booty was transported home, rinsed and liberally garnished with lemon juice and olive oil. Finally, we were ready for the tasting.

The first impact on the tongue was salty. But then, rolling and mashing the roe in my mouth, an iridescent rainbow of tastes shot out and blended into one another in breathtaking profusion: sweet crab, sour citrus, bitter liquor, meaty wild mushrooms, searing horseradish . . . it felt as though I had chewed through a kitchenful of food. The sticky essence lingered for an eternity, transforming, coalescing, then mutating again all the way down the resonant tunnel of my throat. I was in shock. I felt drained, my body post-orgasmic in its stupor. I felt full to bursting. I could not bear the thought of any other food. I wanted to be alone. As I struggled to focus on the others, I realized there was silence at the table, a rare event for my boisterous host family. I wasn't the only one transported by this magical food.

We admired the effortless local beauty and pledged to hunt down more sea urchins the next day. But clearly our luck had run out and I left Greece without tasting that wondrous food again. Once in a while that rainbow of tastes re-ignites on my tongue, bringing my vivid initiation into Greek pleasures rushing back, and I thank the Greek Gods for fate, chance, destiny and the sacred talent of sensual enjoyment.

AFTER READING EXTENSIVELY ON THE
TRAINS AROUND EUROPE, R. ILAYNE
RETURNED TO A CAREER IN RARE BOOK
DEALING. HER WORK HAS BEEN PUB-
LISHED IN A NUMBER OF LITERARY
MAGAZINES.

DOUBTING TAMAS
R. ILAYNE

July 13

It was like a scene from one of those old European movies: I was
surrounded by huge old women with wrinkled breasts, cellulite
legs, heavy stomachs, beautiful faces, all nude. It was in the Hotel
Gellert in Budapest. Someone said something about a bathing cap,
but I had none and instead used my scarf to tie up my hair. It
worked, because the oldest of the bunch gave me an "A-Okay" sign
with her fingers and smiled. I wonder how I looked to them.

Last night I spent a little time with this guy, Tamas, from the youth
hostel. He is more attractive than at first glance – strong jaw, blond
hair, solid-looking body, blue eyes which slant up at the corners,
nice lips that are not too full. I realized that people take on a
different persona in another language. Tamas is much more
spirited when he speaks Hungarian. He gets frustrated, he
says, when he understands everything but can't find the
words for his own thoughts. I feel like an idiot American for
only speaking one language – all the people here know at
least three.

Budapest is one of the most beautiful cities I've ever seen, with
huge old buildings, castles stretching up into the mountains,
statues reaching out of nowhere. So cheap, too! The baths

HUNGARY

cost me $1.50, and the room (which I have to myself), with hot shower and breakfast, less than $5. Incredible! The people have such gentle faces and delicate features. Their language reminds me of something plucked from a mandolin. The only problem is that the mosquitoes are vicious. I have the hugest bites ever all over my hands and legs.

Last night, we saw a few Gypsies – in the metro. Tamas tried to tell me that though he feels sorry for them, "they can get work if they really want to." I'm not so sure about that. Meanwhile, he might know of a job for me. There's a guy from Chicago teaching English here. I'll see. Maybe if it's good, I'll stay.

There are some stained-glass windows right next to me, above a statue of a woman with her arms open. It's neat how nobody ever guesses I'm American, but assume Spanish or Italian, even with my hair getting lighter in the summer sun. The other day in an old movie theatre, I glanced into a big mirror along the staircase, and didn't recognize myself in the dotted black dress that Jeanne gave me – skinny and innocent with such big eyes. I look so young.

Later

> *Why does a gesture, a walk,*
> *stir your blood? What a*
> *mystery this is, desire. The*
> *love sickness, the sensitivity,*
> *the obsession, the flutter of*
> *the heart, the ebb and flow of*
> *the blood. There is no drug or*
> *alcohol equal to it.*
>
> – Anaïs Nin

It's pouring outside. Last night I was thinking about the people I've loved with all my heart. How will I ever get over you, A.? I never would have come here if we stayed together, but why can't I stop thinking of you?

3:50 p.m.

Back at the hostel, after a delicious bowl of mushroom soup and some apple juice from a tiny little bar in the castle district I'll never be able to find again. My ears are still sort of clogged – what's with this cold? At least most of the pressure in my head is gone. I feel much better today, well-rested.

When I went into the lobby, the girl at the desk threw up her hands and said, "Och, this guy – Tommy – said to wait for him." So here I sit.

4:45 p.m.

Still waiting. More Anaïs:

> *There are very few human
> beings who receive the truth,
> complete and staggering, by
> instant illumination. Most of
> them acquire it fragment by
> fragment, on a small scale by
> successive developments,
> cellularly, like a laborious
> mosaic.*

Tell me about it. So often, I think, *yeah*, so *this* is what life's all about, *now* I've got it, and then of course, it's not.

8:35 p.m.

We all went out to dinner. It was fun, but I couldn't understand a word. I'm so attracted to Tamas, keep catching myself wondering what he'd be like. He hasn't tried a thing, all he does is touch me around the waist as a quick greeting, or edge me into a seat on the bus, but what zings in my hips!

July 14

Just finished some rounds of solitaire, thought of conversations I could be having. How I'd love to have lunch with Jane in her backyard, go to the beach with my parents, eat Mexican food with Jackie, stop by and surprise Eric at his father's house. Or just spend time alone, drinking lemon water on the patio and reading a book. I wish I had people around me to listen to my stories.

July 15

We did it. Can you believe he's nineteen years old!!! Acted his age in bed – all style and flower, without true passion. He couldn't wait – this was something to reach, rather than experience. He's still sleeping, facing the wall with his butt sticking all the way out. He wanted to go downstairs, cause he "never sleeps comfortably" with others, but said he would "do [me] this favor" and stay. Thanks.

He was quite clear that this was just sex for him, and that he was really doing it so that I would help him get a job in the States next year. I told him he was an asshole, but maybe he's just straightforward. No romance, no poetry, no passion. What am I looking for, anyway?

July 16

Wow – it's been really strange these last couple of days. My mind has changed about Tamas – the kind of person he is, the kind of guy he appears to be. I thought it would be just a fuck, but I think he has some weird shit going on. When we were walking around yesterday, he seemed so cold – hardly talked, hardly touched. It was difficult, especially since we'd slept together the night before. But then he insisted on helping me go to the university to see if I could find out about teaching jobs, even though I kept telling him that I was just curious. He insisted that he wanted to help me because he wants to come to the States next year and would like some "quid pro quo."

He took me out to Burger King for lunch, a luxury here. He's doing me all these favors, but I can't figure out if he really likes me all that much. And I'm all moody too, since I have my period. I feel like crying for no reason, even had to turn my face away in the restaurant. I wanted to find the way back by myself, but then he got upset ('cause I was?) and put his head in his hands. I was watching his body, and could see his heart pounding through his shirt, fast and hard, and it looked almost like he was shuddering a little, but then he looked up and smiled, and his voice was fine. Strange guy.

July 18

Last night I went to his house in the country, the little town where he's from. Four or five of his friends were waiting at the station, and they all just spoke Hungarian. Two of them were drunk, sweaty and smelly. Tamas paid for the bus, saying nothing. All the way there I tried to hold back the lump in my throat. I looked outside at the sunflowers rushing past and thought about how much I missed my friends – having no one to laugh with in my own language, and having to suffer through other people's plans, like barbecues at strangers' houses.

When we got there, I went to the bathroom to wash my hands and face, and then Tamas showed me their huge garden. It looked like a mini plantation! I saw radishes as big as small pumpkins, zucchini and squash six times their regular size, tasted fruits I don't even know the names of, ate right from the trees. Everything was so fresh – his grandmother killed a chicken for our dinner! I met a little old Hungarian woman in a cornfield and took her picture, and a weathered, tanned Hungarian man, another neighbor, who kissed my hand and insisted I take photos of myself and him with a baby rabbit and white pigeon.

Then Tamas, his friends and I went to a drive-in to see *Stop or My Mom Will Shoot* – not my choice – which of course was in Hungarian. He decided that he preferred to sit outside and talk with his friends, asked if I wanted to come, but I was so tired of not understanding that I said no. Besides, it was so cold and I finally made some excuse to go to the bathroom and ended up taking a fifteen-minute walk up the road by myself in the dark.

"I hope he's worried," I kept thinking, 'cause I felt like shit. I walked up the path in the dark, turned around and looked up at that beautiful orange-white moon dancing in the sky, and the stars, and though the voices from the drive-in carried loudly into echoes all around me, I suddenly relaxed, felt good, kicked the dirt and rocks beneath my sneakers, and energy burst inside me so that I went catapulting up the road further, until I realized that if for some reason the movie ended and I couldn't find them, there would be no way for me to get anywhere – I had no money, didn't speak Hungarian, had no knowledge of Tamas's town or even his last name, no phone number because they had no phone, no way back to Budapest for my backpack, nothing – so I calmed down and stood in the moonlight, listening, waiting to see when and if the movie theme music changed, so that if I had to, I could run back in a hurry and try to locate their car.

When I headed back to the parking lot, they were searching the area. Tamas came up and yelled at me for disappearing, but I was secretly glad, and told him that I was going back to finish my walk. He made me promise to be back within ten minutes, so I went flying back up the road and found a place to cry – something I'd desperately needed to do for so long. I felt so lonely. I cried at not being able to cry in the four months since A. had said it was over, cried at not loving anyone anymore. I cried just for the pleasure of feeling the tears drop from my face and soak the dirt below. I felt them on my fingertips, melting into the sand. It was over too soon, as all the positive thoughts interrupted, how lucky I am to be here, all of that. Then I realized that the movie had ended and ran back.

This morning, I got up to a delicious breakfast. In Hungary, they *feed* you! Salami, rolls, cheese, sausages stuffed with rice, apple juice, butter – yum! Then we took a long walk into the fields, the hills, the forest, saw streams and barking dogs. I learned that "burning needle" is the term for stinging nettle, and I got stung, a little. Here the flies stick to you like salt – they wait on your arms and legs. I drank from two natural springs, and felt my calf muscles blossom as we climbed up this little mountain. At the top, Tamas tried to touch me, but got upset because I hadn't brought my shiny American condoms, and he'd forgotten too, so we just lay with our shirts off on this tiny blanket no bigger than a towel. He tried to kiss my ear where I am most ticklish, and drew a funny rabbit on my leg. I don't know what the hell he was trying to do, though, because as soon as it started getting comfortable, he ruined it, the usual head games – let's go back, no sex, no touching ever again. So we walked back down. At first, I got annoyed, but I think I'm learning that he says the opposite of what things are.

When we got back to the house, lunch was so delicious. I watched him eat a chicken's foot – his little sister got a huge kick out of the look on my face - and then it seemed all better. We all smiled a lot, and I thought, oh, maybe I'll stay. His family is so gracious. They even let me wear their slippers (*papuc*)!

Last day
My train goes back to Budapest in half an hour. I'm really going. Tamas and I said our goodbyes in his room. He's definitely coming to the States, he says, but who knows when. We agreed that it would be great if when we're older and we have our families and children, we can visit each other in our different countries, raise our kids as friends. That will be my little contribution to world peace.

"INSIDE THE CHERRIES" WAS FIRST
READ ON OREGON PUBLIC RADIO AND
MONITORADIO. SANDRA DORR NOW
LIVES IN SOUTHWESTERN COLORADO,
WHERE SHE CLIMBS CANYONS WITH HER
HUSBAND AND CHILDREN, AND DREAMS
OF REVISITING EUROPE.

INSIDE THE CHERRIES

SANDRA DORR

A dream of faraway love sent me to Italy aboard a blue-and-white ocean liner, the *Il Raffaello*. How could I not go? My mother used to sit on the porch in the spring sun, turning the pages of travel magazines while we dove off the swings into the mud. She muttered peculiar words: *Padova, Rio de Janeiro, España, Morocco.*

I was certain a secret, passionate romance went on between my mother and my father, who kissed her once a day in front of us before picking up his lunch bucket and closing the door. I collected the nickels for the dusty box of chocolate-covered cherries we bought our parents every Valentine's Day at Rexall Drug for forty-nine cents plus tax. We glued paper hearts on the box and giggled outside their bedroom, waking them up early to give it to them. They thanked us and usually each ate one, so we brought the box back to the kitchen and divided up the chocolates nestled in layers of rustling paper. The sweet white syrup tasted strangely rich so early in the morning.

Aboard the *Il Raffaello*, I found myself eating chocolates at midnight among a crowd of dark-eyed, dark-haired people who saw this supper as merely a break in a night of dancing. My student ticket allowed me all the privileges of the first-class passengers, except that my cabin was located deep in the ship, next to the engines. Who could sleep? As soon as I stepped aboard, a long-lashed boy of fifteen showed me my

124

tiny bed, then stood in the doorway and offered to visit me that night, with wine.

"Salvadore," I said, "you are the age of my little brother. Beat it." He wailed down the hall, "*Mi dispiace! Mi dispiace!*" I am sorry! I am sorry! All over the ship people slammed doors and screamed and cried. The couple above me fought daily. She would retreat to the deck, hurling insults, until he'd burst into the dining room waving his fists and shouting to us all, "*Puttana! Puttana!*" By midnight they'd be back on the floor, cha-cha-cha-ing, laughing and pinching each other.

I always knew when my parents fought, because my mother took a walk, usually to Rexall Drug. My only taste of love had been the promise I'd made to a sweet engineering student before leaving Minnesota – a promise that disappeared into the waves of the Atlantic when I met Aldo.

He was a creamy-eyed, curly-haired waiter my age who bent over my right shoulder to serve supper. My heart thumped at the V of his warm brown chest under his cuffed white shirt and black ruffled jacket. "I come to your cabin," he said into my hair, his words dark and sweet, his breath light against my sleeveless dress. "Eight o'clock. I bring wine."

For six days we floated through the territory of love, meeting secretly in my cabin when he got off work, or under blankets on a deck chair to watch the stars. Mostly he talked to me about his home, a hill town north of Naples. He couldn't make a living there, so he'd gone to work on the ocean liner.

"It is our life," he said, pulling his jacket from my shoulders. "We all leave Italia, and then we come home."

The day the boat docked in Naples, Aldo got a message to call his mother. He gripped my hand and took me through the city, past thousands of eyes, motorcycles, crumbling stone walls, domes, arches and street latrines, people yelling, children selling ciga-rettes. He went into a post office to make a long-distance call, and when he came out he was crying like a child. We went up to a hill above the city, under oak trees, and he put his head in my lap.

His father had died while we were on the ship.

After a while he tried to explain how he felt. A father, he whispered, a father is almost a *mother*, endowing that word with the weight of the soft green hills around us. Then he ripped off his jacket and swore he would never work on the sea again.

That was our good-bye. Not until I had been away from home for two years did I come to realize that I loved my country as he loved his, that love, ah, *amore*, did not come all at once, but was a place in the heart that recognized home in another, and did not stay the same, but dissolved over and over again, the way the heart beats.

SARAH GOODWIN HAS LIVED IN
GREECE, FINLAND AND GERMANY,
AMONG OTHER EUROPEAN COUNTRIES.
ON RARE OCCASIONS BACK IN HER
NATIVE SEATTLE, SHE WORKS AS A
WRITER AND FREELANCE EDITOR.

PROSE OF PARIS

SARAH GOODWIN

The dormitory was filled with younger students who all seemed to know each other. They preferred the places that other tourists went to: the Eiffel Tower or Champs-Élysées. I was searching for the perfect smoky jazz club with no signs, the hangings of obscure artists' work, the little restaurant off the Seine with a Breton grandmother preparing scrumptious crepes.

Paris's streets twist drunkenly, not like Manhattan's numbered and orderly avenues. One rainy Sunday morning I wandered into a church where the ceilings reached for God. A grand pipe organ played, deep and larger than some buildings. The voices of choir and congregation joined. Closing my eyes, I knew that the church remembered the thousands of voices that had echoed here.

Though it was drizzling, I decided to head for the Luxembourg Gardens. I was absorbed in my tiny laminated street map when an angel came to me.

"You are lost," he said in French I barely understood. "I've been watching you search your little map."

His name was Bruno. He was blue-eyed, red-haired, sweet-faced. He carried a flute.

Who says the muse is a woman? He stood in front of me smiling in a green velvet jacket.

"It does nothing but rain in this horrible city!"

PARIS

"You are wrong," Bruno said. "Paris has beautiful weather."

As if to prove it, out came the sun. We strolled through the Luxembourg beside flowering trees, Greek marble lovers and splashing fountains.

Bruno was as pretty as a girl. In America he would've been ruined. Spreading his jacket on the grass for us to lay on, he hand-rolled a cigarette.

"Only for a minute," he warned. "It is illegal to sit on the grass. If police come, you speak, and they will think we are both American."

That night we found the perfect seedy jazz club where boys banged bongos and played horns. I wished I could draw them, their quick hands, thick necks, African ancestry. We took a boat ride on the Seine, spilling Bordeaux while the lights on the river danced. *Summertime – and the living is easy* . . .

Bruno was the perfect Parisian lover: indolent and elegant. His flat was beautiful, eclectic, filled with fragrant plants, driftwood and bright, open bulbs. Huge windows overlooked Paris's low, slated rooftops.

His grand bed was surrounded by mirrors. One night, while naked, I stared at myself, myself in Paris. Instead of going out into the city, I opened wide the windows and let Paris into me. Inspiration, I decided, comes only after a good meal, good wine, and love from a man, dog, star or open window.

As the pleasant, naked French boy played his flute, his long, hollow notes carried over warm breezes that nuzzled our hair. I looked out at the stars over Paris, inhaling deeply the scent of Bruno's roses into my bright, living flesh. I was wildly aware that I was becoming the person I would be forever.

Matt Sharpe

The Paris debate

It seems that Paris is one of those cities that you either love or hate. It really all depends on what kind of person you are, and what you are looking for out of a visit there. If you are simply there to see the overcrowded sights, make no effort to speak French, and expect the same as you would at home, then forget it – it can be a bad experience. But if you go to the city to experience what the "real" Paris has to offer – laid-back cafés, fresh pastries, French cuisine and wines, the back streets of Marais or Bastille, and doing as the Parisians do in the parks and gardens – then it can be a very different experience. Yes, it is a world city with all that goes with it – the crowds, the dirt, the grind – but that's true of any big city. Paris has something else, however, that you won't find in London or New York. A Gallic attitude to life that enlivens the city, and if you spend the time and effort to understand that, then it can be a fantastic place.

175% Page:

LYNN SCHMEIDLER'S WORK HAS
APPEARED IN A VARIETY OF PUBLI-
CATIONS. SHE FINALLY DID HOOK UP
WITH HER SUPERMAN, AND SOON AFTER
BIRTHED TWO CHILDREN. HER MOST
RECENT TRAVEL ADVENTURE REVOLVED
AROUND SEARCHING FOR DIAPER-RASH
OINTMENT IN THE ENGLISH LAKE
DISTRICT.

CAFFE SUPERMAN

LYNN SCHMEIDLER

Traveling in Europe for the first time, I was not overly concerned about the perils of international trains. The requisite hidden canvas pouch hung from a string around my neck with my passport, traveler's checks and names of emergency contacts. Having not spent the money on a sleeping compartment for the thirteen-hour trip, I was most concerned with whether I would be able to stretch my legs onto the seat across from me.

When the train left the Gare de Lyon, the compartment's one other passenger took her bag and left after realizing she'd chosen a non-smoking car. A man in a thin gray wool coat looked in, frowned and moved on. Afterwards, it was only the conductor who brusquely told me to keep my ticket stub and to remove my heels from the seat.

I was resting my head with my legs again outstretched on the seat opposite, when the door to the compartment opened and a middle-aged woman entered carrying a tattered, over-stuffed bag. She was followed by a man wearing a hat. I pulled my feet in and they sat across from me. The woman placed the bag on the floor between her splayed feet and mumbled something to the man, who shook his head. Then she reached into her bag and took out a package wrapped in wax paper, which she attempted to press into the man's hands. He immediately pushed it back and the bundle tumbled into her lap. A piece of limp lettuce fell to the floor.

FLORENCE

130

I buried my head beneath the pillow as a stream of footsteps tripped outside my door. When a loud car horn broke through my dreams, I jumped up, hoping I had not overslept. It was 11:20.

I hastily brushed my teeth in the little sink in the corner of the room, and dug into the bottom of my bag to pull out a clean shirt. Then I checked the address of the Caffe Superman once more, threw the guidebook on the bed and made my way down the stairs and onto the street.

The day was clear and warm and filled with the odor of fresh bread and exhaust. There were puddles in the gutters of the side streets from where store owners had tossed pails of water. The stones of the buildings were worn and smooth, reminding me of my grandmother's hand holding a magnifying glass over the obituaries, illuminating the names of the dead and who survived them. On the ground ahead of me I saw something sparkling and reached down to pick up a piece of gold ribbon. It seemed an auspicious sign. I slipped it around my hair and tied it in a little knot at the base of my neck.

Rounding the corner of Via Bufalini I pulled in my stomach and glanced at my reflection in a shop window, straightening my posture. My pulse beat at my throat.

I arrived first. It was a small place with a relatively busy bar. Sitting at a table near the door, I ordered an espresso. It was 11:55. Men and women came in and out, ordering cappuccinos, downing sandwiches and leaving. Behind me, a couple of English-speaking students complained about how long it had been since their last bagel. Two elderly men sat at the table to my right, silently playing chess.

I took tiny sips of my coffee, so as not to appear to have been there too long. By 12:20, I'd finished it and ordered another. Neal must have underestimated the time it would take to walk here, I thought, only slightly concerned. At 12:40 I asked for a *pane cioccolatto* and had to rebuff a seedy-looking guy with bad teeth. He's overslept, I told myself, determined not to think the worst. At 1:15, with too much caffeine in my body and a knot of undigested pastry in my stomach, I left.

Outside in the warm, pungent air, I dodged the people around me in a kind of jittery haze. My nails dug into my palms. Walking down the street, I tried to place the blame somewhere – on his age, on mine, on the wiles of Italy or the cruelty of fate. It took all my will to stop my eyes from washing with tears, to keep my legs from collapsing beneath me, to breathe without gulping.

It was about three blocks down that I saw him sitting at an outdoor table at a café on the corner. My first impulse was to turn and bolt, but he saw me, so I continued towards him until I stood in front of him. Uncrossing my arms from beneath my breasts, I gave a little wave.

"How you doing?" I asked, impressively casual.

"Okay," he said tentatively. The sunlight reflected off the spoon in his hand, blinding me for a moment.

"Well, see you around," I uttered as I blinked and turned away. No need to prolong the awkwardness. There was no scene.

A few days later, I was looking for a shortcut to the Piazza della Signoria, when I found myself again on Via Bufalini. Just ahead of me was the café where I'd stumbled upon Neal. A young German couple were arguing at the table where he'd sat. Something on the ground ahead caught my eye, and I stooped to pick up the gold ribbon I'd tied in my hair the other morning. As I rose, a man's bag knocked into my shoulder. Twisting to regain my balance, I saw the sign in the window. It read, *Caffè Superman II*.

CHAPTER 4

CONNECTION

lost_adventure
(2 replies)

Where do you learn the most?

Recently in Rome, I found myself unable to get excited about the centuries of art and history found in that city's monuments and museums. Instead, I found myself sitting in my hotel room, reading books about wars, or looking at maps showing the area of the Roman Empire at its mightiest. Other days I find looking out a train window teaches me more about a culture than visiting its museums.

How about you?

megpatterson
1.

No David

I just returned from three weeks in Florence and did not see the *David* there. Every day I almost did it . . . but got occupied looking out the rented apartment's window at women hanging clothes on the lines outside their windows. I tried to figure out who lived in each apartment by the laundry hung on the line . . .

Then I rented a scooter. I wanted to be part of the movement and motion and crazy loudness of the city. It was scary at first, but I got better at it. I figured I would ride my scooter over to the Academy and see the David . . . nope. Just renting it was a cultural experience though: the rental place I had emailed was never open during its posted hours . . . so I had to learn to use the telephone . . . and wait. I spent three days hanging out on the street where the scooter place was, watching workmen fix a roof, buying juice glasses in a hardware store, learning how to order fresh pasta in Italian, looking at books and paper and pottery and trying not to be cold while sitting on the stone steps of the rental place. The actual rental was a quick affair: "Sure you can ride" and a push out into the traffic. I stuck to making only right-hand turns for the first three days. I thought the bike would make my wanderings more efficient; instead I got lost a lot on one-way streets, and since locking up the bike was a big deal, I often chose to just keep going. But I did find the Museum of Science and looked at Galileo's telescopes and his embalmed middle finger. I also checked out the wax carvings of pregnant bellies bearing all kinds of babies in all kinds of difficult predicaments. So the Florentines were delving way "in" and way "out" at the same time. What a great time – I wonder if there is any of that spirit of inquiry left? Maybe next time I'll see *David*.

redcanvas
2.

You only learn if you want to!

I went to Rome once . . . and although I appreciated that everything was really old . . . and beautiful and had tons of history . . . I was hard pressed to find a publication that could do it justice. It's hard. Since then I have taken a few history courses at university and learned about things that I saw . . . but had no idea what they were at the time. Now I'm ready to go back and fully appreciate the experience! So . . . my answer to your question is learn about the things at your own pace . . . you're not going to learn about anything if you don't want to . . . it's gotta be fun.

LORI HORVITZ'S WORK HAS BEEN PUB-
LISHED IN A VARIETY OF LITERARY
JOURNALS AND ANTHOLOGIES. AFTER
HER FIRST TRIP, SHE WAS STRUCK BY
WANDERLUST AND HAS SINCE TRAV-
ELED THROUGHOUT EUROPE, RUSSIA,
CHINA AND MEXICO.

NAKED HIPPIES
AND BONFIRES

LORI HORVITZ

I met Maria, a 25-year-old ex-junkie from Copenhagen, on a kibbutz located just outside of Nazareth. Like me, she had come to
volunteer. During our late-night jam sessions, Maria would sometimes take the spotlight and sing "Summertime" or Eric Clapton's
"Wonderful Tonight." Mostly, though, she encouraged me to play
my guitar, telling me how talented I was, how I'd be famous one
day. And who should know better than her?

"Before the heroin," she told me, "I studied music at university.
I've given recitals." On occasion, we'd sneak into the kibbutz
school and Maria would sit at the piano, take a deep breath, and
begin to sweep her long fingers across the keyboard, playing
Chopin, Bach, Vivaldi. Her renditions left me breathless.

Never before had I met such a powerful woman, someone
so talented and glamorous, in a young Katherine Hepburn,
movie-star kind of way. I couldn't believe it when she told me
she had worked as a prostitute in Copenhagen. "To support
my addiction," she said. Her clients included politicians, rock
stars and rich businessmen.

Before she got kicked off the kibbutz, we made plans to
meet on the isle of Crete. And so, thirty days later, I stepped
onto a gigantic ship bound for Greece, spreading my sleeping
bag on its deck. A tall, bronze-skinned man lay claim to the
space beside me, and offered up bread, cheese and chocolate.

ISTANBUL

That night, I pulled out my guitar and sang my repertoire of songs as a group of fans begged for more, including the beautiful Dutchman beside me. The next night, we held each other, laughed together and had our first kiss. What more could I want at nineteen?

When we arrived in Iraklio, Crete's port, Maria and her new friend, Sue, were waiting. We took bus after bus, then walked a mile to finally arrive at a tucked-away beach dotted with naked hippies and bonfires. The four of us claimed a small cove, our home for the week. Maria showed us how to make pita bread from flour, water and jelly, rolled out with a wine bottle. At night, we'd join the hippies, play music and watch the sun set over the pounding ocean.

After a week of this paradise, we took a ship to Athens, visited ruins, then embarked on a 24-hour bus ride to Istanbul, with no toilet to speak of. At one point, I peed into a plastic bag and threw it out the window.

In Istanbul, we negotiated with a hotel owner to sleep on his roof for the equivalent of fifty cents a night. The panorama of mosques and minarets encircling us was awesome. As we explored the city, there were a lot of stares directed at us: the alluring Danish ex-prostitute, the voluptuous Brit, the handsome Dutchman and me, a curly-haired Jew dressed in loose-fitting Arabic clothing. Often, I brought my camera up to eye level and took pictures of the men around us, but they never changed their blank expressions.

One morning, after the others had left, the Dutchman and I remained on the roof under our sleeping bags. For the first time since meeting, we shed all our clothes and fumbled atop each other, our bodies sweaty and goosebumped. Afterwards, arms wrapped loosely about each other, I heard a cough. Turning my head, I caught sight of two Turkish boys, no more than eleven years old, standing on the roof's ledge about ten yards away. Even after my eyes met theirs, they didn't flinch.

Right down the road from our hotel was an infamous café where travelers and drug dealers hung out. We patronized this place at least once a day for coffee, alcohol or a bowl of soup.

That was where something changed for Maria. I didn't question her sudden lethargy at first, but later discovered that one of the men at the café was offering her heroin for her services. Maria even began to rent a separate room where she could entertain her clients.

One day, when the four of us went to the Grand Bazaar to buy clothes, she disappeared.

"She just stole one of my jackets!" one of the shop owners exclaimed a few minutes later.

"We just met her," the Dutchman lied. "We don't even know her name."

"If I don't get that jacket back," the shop owner shouted, pointing his finger at us, "I'll call the police and have you all arrested."

My friends shifted their weight as beads of sweat appeared on Sue's forehead. But I found the whole situation exciting.

"Why don't you two stay here? I'll see if Maria is at the hotel. If she has the jacket, I'll bring it back."

A few minutes later I knocked on her door, then entered to find her weeping on the bed, the stolen jacket beside her.

"I don't know what's happening to me," she moaned. "I can't control myself."

I put my arm around her shoulder. "I just have to bring back the jacket and then everything will be fine."

The shop owner was more than pleased, and ended up taking us all out to a dinner of kebabs, potatoes, tabouli and Turkish delight. But Maria's drug use was causing serious problems. I suggested we leave Istanbul, the land of cheap heroin. I couldn't stand watching her lose the strength I so admired and learned from. Besides, I had to start making my way to Tel Aviv for the flight home, and the Dutchman had to get back to Amsterdam.

Maria and I took a bus back to Athens, making sure to take enough water, bread, cheese and plastic bags. Her eyes were bloodshot, and moments after opening a can of soft drink, I heard a loud clank: she had fallen asleep and dropped it on the floor. Through slit eyes, she confessed that she still had a little bit of heroin left, but promised that she was done with the drugs after that.

"I want to go back to university," she said, "for music."

In Athens, she saw me off at the port. "Pray for me," she begged. "I really want to quit." We hugged and promised to visit each other, and with my big maroon pack on my back and guitar in hand, I stepped onto the ship.

When I got back to New York, I wrote letters and tried to call. But I never heard from her again. Two years later I visited Copenhagen, but Maria was nowhere to be found.

I like to think she was touring the world, giving recitals in Peking, Sydney and Chicago, her long fingers whipping across the keyboard. And afterwards, with a modest smile upon her face, taking a graceful, dignified bow.

LISA BEATMAN HITS THE ROAD A LOT,
BUT CALLS BOSTON HOME. SHE HAS
BEEN AWARDED TWO RESIDENCIES AND
HAS RECEIVED A MASSACHUSETTS
CULTURAL COUNCIL GRANT.

MARY MCGREGOR

LISA BEATMAN

Narrow, shoulderless roads wound past hills bleating with sheep. With enormous exertion I retrained myself to walk facing traffic on the correct side of an Irish road. Several near misses provided peerless incentive. Halfway to Newbliss, a small Fiat discharged a large, square woman shod in Reeboks and a cardigan, who commenced walking beside me.

"Mary McGregor, I am, and you must be one o' them artists up at Annamakherig. Pleased to meet you," she panted, explaining that she was walking on account of her diabetes, which Dr. Flannerty had ordered she combat with daily walks, but that she was only managing one a week. She was just as bad with the new diet, apparently.

"It's a pity not to end a meal with something sweet," she sighed. Fortunately, quite a few years back, she had given up sugar with her tea for Lent, and never went back. That made it easier, but she still gave in to a biscuit all too often.

"I've been a hairdresser for fifty years; since I was fifteen or sixteen. Isn't that terrible?" Mary's lips turned up, indicating that she didn't think so herself. "There's another one in town, now. A relation – me first cousin – set herself up in opposition; can you imagine?"

Not waiting for me to respond, she continued, "Mind the roads, now." I nodded, about to regale her with harrowing tales of my hometown's infamous drivers. She pointed to the

IRELAND

cattle grazing placidly on the heathered hillside. "Those bulls can be something fierce, I tell you. The farmers tell me that this time of year the bulls are high. I dinna why, they just are. Why, just last month a local man – he was up around eighty but still spry – he was walking this very road when a herd came upon him, the bull walking nice as a cow when suddenly he attacked. That poor man was kil't, and not in one piece. A leg over there and an arm all the way over on the other side of the hedge there, you see, hanging down as if the hand had still enough life in it on the way over to grab hold, hoping that the rest would follow. It didn't, of course. We buried him, poor soul, all we could find."

We had just entered Newbliss proper, and stopped in front of what must have been her shop: yellowish, as she had described, with a small faded sign depicting crossed shears over a beehive hairdo. She invited me to stop by, anytime, and sent me on my way.

"Welcome to Ireland, love, but mind the roads."

MARY ANN LARKIN IS A WRITER OF
PROSE AND POETRY LIVING IN
WASHINGTON D.C. HER WORK HAS
APPEARED WIDELY — *IN POETRY
GREECE, POETRY IRELAND, NEW
LETTERS* AND OTHER PUBLICATIONS.

A LONGING FOR UNION

MARY ANN LARKIN

The air is thick with cigarette smoke and the leashed energy of men's voices. Carolee and I sip our red wine. Here in Sliven, we do not feel the river charm of Ruse or the centuries of Nesebâr dreaming one on top of another. Here, rage simmers just beneath the staccato talk of the ruined faces. The waitress hurries among them, a nurse tending a ward of feverish, wounded men who have decided they have little to lose.

Outside, blue mountains cradle the town and the thousand-year-old oak that shadows the square and redeems it all. The mountains too have nothing to lose. Their silver-blue light is indifferent. It covers everything, offers shelter and danger indiscriminately.

"May I help you?" a man asks, bending over our café table, his body electric beneath the dark T-shirt. Long blond hair and a beard shade his face, except for his brilliant green eyes, which are like hooded ovals of energy.

The waitress pauses impatiently as the man helps us with our order. It is early June and there are few vegetables, only meat and a spring salad, he explains. We order two salads and ask him, as he moves to leave, how it is he speaks such perfect English.

"I studied at university and have done some English translations," he says and moves to rejoin his friends at the next table.

BULGARIA

On his way out, our translator pauses at our table again. "Don't stay here past eight o'clock," he cautions. "The place is full of criminals and would-be criminals." We use his warning as an excuse to leave with him, eager to ask about Bulgaria and the criminals and would-be criminals.

His name is Stefan. He walks with us through the square of the blue mountain town. He will take us to a restaurant where we might find fish and vegetables. "Maybe," he emphasizes. His cigarette flashes back and forth as he answers our questions with a cool politeness. Underneath his formality, I sense eagerness, despair and an intellect sharp as a mountain's peak. An old darkness pulls him down even as hope propels him upward. He seems accustomed to hardship. Only his shoulders hunch protectively against it.

He tells us he is a writer, and we speak of poetry and the vegetables we have not been able to find since our arrival. He talks of speakeasies, break dancing and mysticism. In the restaurant he brings us to, he again helps us order before saying goodbye. But before we finish our meal, he returns. "I have talked to my friends," he begins, "and if you like, we can go now to meet in the studio of one of them. We can talk and read poetry and look at paintings. I will translate."

We accept happily and follow him through now-dark streets to a courtyard gate. We enter and, from the shadows, his friends from the café appear, Atanas and Krum. They greet us graciously and show us into a tiny room. Within are several poets and artists, with names like music. They offer us wine and brandy. But we are all shy; Carolee and I know only a few words of Bulgarian, and Stefan is the only one who speaks English.

Krum hands Stefan the poems of a childhood friend, Elissavetta, and Stefan begins translating, reading them to us in English. Carolee, however, is sleepy, and the artists are restless. Atanas takes charge.

"It is difficult as we have no common language. But no one is to worry. We will read a little, drink, talk and learn about each other. There is time for everything."

They tell us about Elissavetta, the poet who has just left their city. Her absence is a pain among them that has not healed. She lives in Plovdiv now, where we will go in a few days after we visit the Black Sea. They would like us to meet her, and perhaps take her poems to America to publish, but she does not speak English.

Stefan will arrange everything. When Carolee and I arrive in Plovdiv, he will meet us, bring us to Elissavetta and act as translator. Krum and Atanas will also try to come. It is settled.

I tell Stefan that although I would like to try, I am not sure whether I can get Elissavetta's poems published. "It does not matter," he answers. "What matters is that someone knows that something is happening in this Godforsaken country.

"Also, in Plovdiv lives Kosta, an artist who speaks some English," Stefan adds. "But he has an attribute that will interest you more. He is a vegetarian." Stefan's laugh is like the sun striking quartz in a rock.

It is late, and the next day we will travel to the Black Sea. Atanas and Stefan walk us through the dark mountain night to our old hotel.

"We had to spend too much time on arrangements," Atanas says, summing up the evening. "We did not get to know each other deeply. We were not able to speak slowly and honestly of what we felt about matters of importance. But we will meet again."

All the unshared dreams and confidences of our small evening lie stillborn between us as we say good night. Atanas kisses our hands. Stefan is shy.

We will meet on Monday at five at the Plovdiv Restaurant.

Carolee and I stand on the steps of the luxurious Plovdiv Hotel. It is Monday, three o'clock. The sand of the Black Sea scratches at our hearts. The taxi driver, having already taken us to three different hotels, is preparing to leave in disgust.

"We are looking for the Plovdiv Restaurant," I tell the doorman. "Is it in this hotel?"

"We have a restaurant, but it is not called the Plovdiv Restaurant. This is the Plovdiv Hotel," he answers, "but it is a fine restaurant and hotel. May I take your bags?" He speaks patiently, as if to a young child. "There is no Plovdiv Restaurant in this city."

I wonder if he thinks I believe there is only one restaurant in Plovdiv. Picturing Stefan and Elissavetta betrayed, I tell him our story. A small crowd gathers. Deciding not to move until someone tells us where the Plovdiv Restaurant is, I put down my bag. Carolee stands beside me with her backpack and black straw hat, smiling dreamily.

"Our friends said everyone in town knows it," I direct my remarks to the doorman. "Artists exhibit paintings there."

"There is a place," he hesitates. "Do your friends have beards and long hair?"

"Yes," I say. Our taxi driver leaves.

"There is a rough place where drunkards sit drinking from morning till night. I think I have seen a few paintings there. But it is a pub, not a restaurant."

"That's it, I think."

"Well, this taxi driver can take you," he says. The onlookers step back, staring and shaking their heads.

"But please write down the address in case we get lost again."

"It is not necessary. Everyone knows where it is," he answers. "I will be here until eleven tonight, if you need me," he calls after us.

Carolee and I pile our bags around our chairs in the Plovdiv Pub. It is not quite five. We order red wine and spring salads. The drunkards, with their beautifully ruined faces, drink politely around us.

At five, Stefan enters in his thin black T-shirt, followed by Elissavetta. She is red and black and white: her dark hair like a curved Prince Valiant cap; her skirt, earrings and lips bright red against milky skin. There is something of the moon about her.

They order brandy. We chat, all a little shy. Atanas and Krum could not come, they tell us. We tell them of our adventures in Nesebâr – how the militia came to our house because Carolee was writing in public.

"We hope your policemen are brighter than ours," Stefan laughs.

Elissavetta tells us how she met Krum in a summer camp for good students. They both wrote poetry there, but now no editor will publish their work.

Elissavetta wants to learn English, but Stefan will not teach her. "She would not be a good student," he claims, his eyes turning tender as he laughs beneath her indignant gaze. Being a translator suits Stefan. He does not change a shade of meaning, and is able to say all of the words that go off in his head like firecrackers.

Although Kosta, the artist and vegetarian, has made hotel reservations for us, Elissavetta invites us to stay at her house. We accept, but Stefan is not happy.

"I think," he says, "you must stay at the hotel. Her neighbors will talk, and she might have trouble with the militia and end up on a list."

No one wants to be on the lists. We hastily agree.

With Stefan carrying our bags, we leave the Plovdiv Pub to find Kosta, who is waiting outside. He is exceedingly tall and beautiful, yet quick-moving; the hub around which the illicit artistic life of the city revolves. He has arranged everything.

A little before seven, Stefan and I walk through Plovdiv's wide square to meet the poets and artists that are his friends. Carolee will not come. She is entranced with our grand hotel, and will go to bed early to dream.

We turn into a courtyard and up many flights of ramshackle stairs to Kosta's studio. Elissavetta is there with a Buddha-like husband, and Kosta, and a tiny lawyer who announces to me that he knows exactly three hundred words of English.

Kosta's dreamlike watercolors surround us. We gather around a wooden table as the warm night air drifts into the room through an open window. Kosta talks quietly without stopping. He brings out white cheese, a dish of cold cabbage, tomatoes, peppers and brown bread, and pours large glasses of brandy for everyone. Chocolates appear.

Stefan, too, is very busy. He is our link. We are all quietly excited, yet apprehensive, about the evening before us. I do not remember how we began, the first serious or humorous words, or the moment when we all realized we were held together by our deep longing for union.

The evening becomes infinite, as we float together above the night-falling city. Our masks dissolve and we put on the faces we reserve for solitude, listening with the intensity of the blind tapping their way through new streets.

Stefan works hard, grabbing the English words he wants desperately, as though panning for gold in a stream bed almost dry. We talk of each other's countries and poems. They are prisoners hungry for news and I am a starving pilgrim from a land where people move so fast their words are lost. Our common need lies between us, both wound and gift.

They want their poems to be heard, their paintings to be seen. But their all-powerful editors pick and choose according to some invisible power that has nothing to do with purity of word and form. I tell them that in my country, literature is of so little consequence that it seems not to exist for those in power.

Stefan translates some of Elissavetta's poems into English. It is his biggest challenge. In his passion for clarity, he gulps his brandy and tears at his hair. "My English is deserting me," he moans, like an abandoned lover. Soon the poems drift among us in two languages, delicate and strong, part of an ancient line of longing voices and airborne questions.

Elissavetta will not give me her poems to take to America as Stefan wants her to do. "She writes in Bulgarian. She wants to be published here," Stefan translates.

They ask for my poems. Stefan translates some about America, about the Potomac.

"These are very pantheistic," says Kosta. I try to tell him how important nature is to an American – our dominant force – yet how we turn on it now, after we have conquered it, like greedy teenagers.

"We know this. We know this," says Stefan. He and Kosta speak of America's lost purpose, our floundering. They quote writers they have read.

"Is there no one with a vision to lead America?" Kosta asks.

I tell them there is no such leader with a vision of world peace and unity.

The evening is like long, slow lovemaking. We move in and out of each other's orbits. When we need to breathe, we go to the window for air, and also to see if we still exist separately, or if the world we are making has swallowed us.

Elissavetta walks over to stand beside me at the open window. "I cannot speak English," she says sadly.

"*Az ne razbiram Bulgarski*, Elissavetta," I answer, putting my arm around her. She leans her head on my shoulder, and for just a moment, we stand together at the window, the city at our feet.

Kosta leans toward me and Stefan translates his words. "What do you believe in? What do you hope for?"

I try to convey what it is I believe in, but it is such a difficult question that I find it hard to put my thoughts into words. "I believe," I finally tell them, "that we must create ourselves and through ourselves the world. That we must be strong enough and brave enough to claim this responsibility as our own. But you must tell us what to hope for, Kosta."

"Well," he answers, "if we are to create the world, we must hope to see clearly what it is we are meant to do and to do it well. We must hope, too, that we can help each other."

Stefan translates so carefully. We are all very still as we listen to Kosta.

The sounds of the city are still now. The air is thick with night. The chocolates are gone and the cabbage and cheese. Only my brandy remains.

It is long past midnight. Outside, the main promenade of the city is empty. Only a few workers pull hoses behind them; mammoth sea serpents watering away the day's dust and dreams.

We enter the night air as though rising from underwater. Bits of each other – gestures, and words spoken and unspoken – cling to us still; seaweed from a richer world.

MARJORIE MADDOX, A PROFESSOR OF
ENGLISH AT LOCK HAVEN UNIVERSITY,
HAS PUBLISHED SIX COLLECTIONS OF
POETRY AND MORE THAN 250 POEMS IN
LITERARY JOURNALS. SHE LOVES TO
WRITE, READ AND TRAVEL WITH HER
HUSBAND AND TWO SMALL CHILDREN —
EVEN IF IT'S ONLY AROUND THE
BLOCK.

DANCING ITALIAN

MARJORIE MADDOX

In Venice, a man we just met
picks at his instrument, starts to hum
while you lean on a chipped statue,
strum your borrowed guitar
before twenty Italians.

An old man asks me to dance,
then tips his tattered sailor's cap.
I step twice to each of his twirls
as his English, his Italian, his wine
all slur to a song he once heard at a local café:
"Joy is everywhere, funiculi, funicula!"
When he mutters "Maria,"
his gray eyes shine.

It is past evening,
the shadows become girls clapping
and somewhere between my spins,
the notes of accordions
swirl in from the canals,
where gondoliers steer couples
until dawn.

VENICE

151

All the while,
though your smile and the statue
and the dark faces blur into one,
I step in and out and around
with the old man, timing my steps
to his heart, and the quick beat
of your fingers.

GREG TULEJA HAS WORKED AS A
MUSICIAN, PIANO TECHNICIAN AND
TEACHER. HE IS NOW ACADEMIC DEAN
AT A PRIVATE HIGH SCHOOL.

A SLIGHT LEANING BACKWARD

GREG TULEJA

It's not uncommon, when you're young, to gather together a few
dollars, strap on a backpack and spend part of a summer hitchhiking through Europe, searching for unknown foreign adventures or
merely trying to postpone the inevitable adult responsibility called
"work." For those who have just finished college, Europe beckons
irresistibly from across the Atlantic, a powerful magnet to hungry
seekers of romance or naïve pretenders to what is considered cultural enlightenment.

Though I shared some of this inspiration for European travel, I
also had something else in mind, something that gave my first trip
to Europe a unique quality. Unlike my more practical fellow travelers who had scraped together modest but sufficient funds for their
journeys, I had not saved enough money to last the month I hoped
to stay in France. But I had a plan that I thought would set my trip
apart from the rest – I would earn my own way by playing flute in
the subway.

Arriving in Paris with a great deal of formal instruction in
flute but almost no training in French, I settled into one of
several student hotels that lined the rue Sommerard in the
Latin Quarter. It boasted a one-star classification, but I soon
became convinced that absolutely no aspect of the Hotel
Thillois deserved even the smallest fraction. My tiny room
was dark and dismally furnished, with dingy, threadbare bed-

PARIS

153

covers, no windows and an especially unfortunate feature – the closest bathroom was one floor *up,* and the key to that bathroom was two floors *down.*

Yet I was oblivious to this and all other inconveniences – I was in Paris and, to me, that was all that mattered. In that month I discovered that, with a little bit of effort, the necessary adjustments to a new culture could be made quite comfortably. The trip turned out to be a great success: my French improved dramatically, I played flute in the Paris metro for money, and I made a friend.

I had brought a music stand from New York and as much sheet music as I could cram into a large leather bag, and on my second day in the city, I set up for business in a bright corner of the Odéon metro station. As I had envisioned in countless dreams, I positioned myself proudly near the end of the platform and began to hit the first notes. The sound of my flute filled the station, and as I played one piece after another, silver coins and the occasional paper note were tossed into my opened case by hurrying French commuters or tourists from Germany or Japan. In addition to the money, I was occasionally rewarded with enthusiastic applause; a thrilling sound that, to my ears, blended beautifully with the screeching of trains entering and leaving the station.

I played for an hour and a half each morning and afternoon, and made thirty or forty francs a day. I was very happy.

Packing up my gear at the end of my fourth day in Paris, I was approached by a neatly dressed young man.

"Hello, my name is Henri Latelle. You play beautifully," he said in English. "Are you an American?"

"*Oui*," I answered stupidly. "I mean, yes, I am."

"I play flute down here too, over at St.-Michel. I think we could make very much money playing duos. All tips divided equally, of course. We could split everything . . . how do you say . . . fifty-fifty?"

"Yes, that's right. Fifty-fifty. Down the middle."

"Down the middle. Yes. Well, what do you say?"

"Well, sure," I told him. "Do you have sheet music? All I brought with me are solo pieces."

"I have plenty of music. I will meet you here tomorrow morning."

"Okay. I've been starting at about ten."

"Oh, yes, I know. I have been listening. I will see you tomorrow."

So began a glorious month of playing music with Henri Latelle. He had a large collection of duets, familiar pieces by Telemann and Kuhlau, and also some French music I had never played – Hotteterre, Naudot, Couperin. Henri's pure joy for making music was infectious, and we performed at first mainly for ourselves, but later for ever-growing crowds of people. We gradually became celebrated fixtures in the Odéon station and made good money, which we usually squandered on food and drink, sometimes accompanied by Henri's fiancée, the elegant, inscrutable Julie.

Henri and Julie had almost reached the distant age of thirty, and to me they seemed terribly sophisticated and experienced. They became my generous, warm-hearted guides to the infinite possibilities that Paris had to offer the first-time visitor. Gracious in their tolerance of my poor French, they were tireless in their efforts to introduce me to the richness and variety of Parisian life. Henri also insisted on paying for every meal, museum or concert. My polite protests to his exasperating generosity became routine.

Only once did I notice Henri glare at Julie with frightening malice. It was the first and only break in equanimity that he revealed during my entire stay in Paris: one crack in a charming facade of repose and good will. Even then Henri seemed to recover immediately, his angry expression fading so suddenly that I remember wondering if I had actually seen it at all. I am sure that I missed other clues – his occasional absences from our morning meetings at Odéon; his odd habit of wearing many layers of clothing, even in the heat of midsummer – and never did I question the yellow pill that Julie offered to him every day, precisely at noon. I was too busy enjoying myself to pay much attention to the suggestion that anything could be wrong.

After a month, summer ended and the time came for me to return to school in New York. We marked the occasion with a sumptuous, three-hour dinner in a small café on the rue des Ecoles, elaborately financed by Henri. Laughing about my frequent mistakes with

French grammar, we recalled some of our favorite moments – apart from making music together – like watching sunsets from the steps of Sacré Coeur, and sailing toy boats at the Luxembourg Gardens. During that last dinner, it occurred to me that in over a month in Paris, I had seen the Eiffel Tower only occasionally from great distances, and had never really gotten a good look at the Arc de Triomphe.

"That's all right, Greg," said Julie. "I have heard that New Yorkers spend their whole lives in Manhattan and never go to the top of the Empire State Building."

"And it will give you a reason to come back," said Henri.

I vowed to do that and Henri promised to visit me in the States. "We will play on the steps of Saint Patrick's Cathedral," he said. "We'll make a murder."

"A *killing*, Henri. We'll make a killing."

"Yes, and then spend it all on a huge dinner in the most expensive restaurant we can find. Big American steaks from Texas. In America, you can pay all the bills."

Close to tears, we exchanged addresses on the rue des Ecoles and said goodbye. I flew home the next day.

About a month later, I sent Henri and Julie a long letter thanking them for their warmth and hospitality, which completely obliterated for me the stereotype of the distant and skeptical Parisian, full of scorn and suspicion towards all Americans.

A few weeks later, Julie replied. It was a short letter, in French, which I laboriously translated with the help of a dictionary.

It is my sad duty to tell you that Henri died last week. I was not present, but there were many witnesses, and the police explained to me what happened. Henri was playing flute in Odéon. Suddenly he stopped, walked to the edge of the platform and turned around. As a train pulled into the station, Henri just leaned backward slightly. It was a small movement, they said, hardly noticeable. A gentle leaning backward, that was all.

Greg, when you were here with us in Paris, I am sure you could see that I was very much in love with Henri. But I should

*also admit that I was sometimes quite afraid of him. Henri was
so unsettled, so unpredictable. But he had a very restful summer
– I think one of the best since I had known him. Meeting you
was good for him, and after you returned home he spoke of you
often, always with fondness. But you were here for only a short
time. You did not see Henri's other side. In many ways, he was
unhappy. Always a little unhappy.*

I thought of Henri's wish to visit New York. That day, out of
some uncertain sense of respect and longing for him, I carried my
flute to Saint Patrick's. For a moment I stood there on the sidewalk, case in hand, but my intended musical gesture somehow did
not seem to be a proper tribute, and in the end I decided not to
play. I could not help but think that if we had played together here
in *my* country, Henri would have been disappointed. I believe
now what I did then: New York is not a place for playing music
on the streets.

MARSHALL KRANTZ WRITES ABOUT
TRAVEL FROM HIS HOME IN OAKLAND,
CALIFORNIA. HIS ESSAYS AND FEATURE
ARTICLES HAVE APPEARED IN THE
*WASHINGTON POST, LOS ANGELES TIMES,
COASTAL LIVING* AND UNITED AIRLINES'
HEMISPHERES, AMONG MANY OTHER
NEWSPAPERS AND MAGAZINES. HE HAS
ALSO CONTRIBUTED TO A NUMBER OF
TRAVEL GUIDEBOOKS.

NOCTURNAL MADRILEÑOS

MARSHALL KRANTZ

Nobody goes to bed in Madrid
until they have killed the night.
Ernest Hemingway

Midnight at the Puerta del Sol, the center of Madrid, the center of Spain, and there's a hellish traffic jam. It's a week night, and it's perfectly normal. And while the traffic-bound Madrileños (people of Madrid) clog the square, their footloose countrymen crowd the sidewalks, working their way from *tasca* to *taberna*, itinerant revelers all.

No doubt the majority of Madrid's three million people turn in at a reasonable hour, as befits proud, hard-working members of the European Union. But the myth, sustained by a healthy dose of reality, persists that Madrid is a city most awake at night – all night. It's not for nothing that Madrileños are called *gatos* (cats), for their nocturnal prowling habits.

Spaniards like to say, politely yet with a whiff of superiority, that Americans live to work but Spaniards work to live. So for this American reared on Puritan values ("early to bed, early to rise . . ." Thanks, Ben), coming to terms with Madrid's *joie de vivre* was not easy, especially when so much of it took place well past my bedtime. Fortunately for me, Madrid nights begin in the afternoon, with a siesta. That's the secret to survival.

SPAIN

In the early evening, I met my companions, and we set off through the narrow streets of Old Madrid in search of *tapas*, the famous Spanish snacks. We didn't have to look far. It seemed that every other storefront housed a bar. Madrid's eating and drinking establishments are so numerous and varied that *Madrileños* cut a fine distinction between them. They call them *tasca*, *taberna*, *meson*, *cervecería*, café or *restaurante*. They even have a separate name for the outdoor cafés that spring to life during the summer: *las terrazas* (the terraces).

We ducked into the first place we chanced upon, a *tasca*. A long, wooden bar dominated the small room. There were no barstools and only a few tables and chairs. Patrons were packed in, wreaking convivial havoc upon the place and themselves with a blizzard of eating, drinking and loud talking. The din was truly impressive. Barely keeping up with the barrage of orders, the bartender furiously worked the beer-tap while another man slapped little plates of *tapas* on the bar: olives, almonds, cured ham, sautéed squid or shrimp, and tortilla española, a quiche-like potato omelette served in slices. It was a clean place, except for the floor just below the bar, which was covered with napkins. Trashing the floor is an old custom, one that keeps boys with brooms employed throughout Madrid.

Madrileños do the *tapas* crawl from about 7 p.m. to 10 p.m., or 11 p.m., or midnight, when it's time for dinner. Or they may just go on snacking and drinking all night. My American companions and I, in fact, chafed at the ceaseless victualing to which our Spanish hosts subjected us. "All we ever do is eat," we complained, failing to understand that eating and drinking are secondary concerns. The main course at any Spanish meal is conversation. In fact, conversation is so important that Madrid institutionalized it long ago. It is called *la tertulia*, meaning social gathering. Friends or colleagues meet regularly to discuss business, politics, art, the art of living, or maybe just to gossip or talk about sports.

After conducting our own impromptu *tertulia*, we moved deeper into Old Madrid, pausing briefly at Plaza de Santa Ana, a small square with a large appetite for partying. The numerous bars around Plaza de Santa Ana attract loads of university students. On this night they spilled out the doors of Cervecería Alemana and onto the plaza. Cervecería Alemana is also traditionally a favorite with bullfight aficionados, so it's no surprise that it was also a haunt of Hemingway.

Fortified once more, we pushed on to Plaza Mayor, Madrid's famous landmark. The rectangular plaza is enclosed by ground-level shops set along arcades, and on the succeeding three floors by seventy-eight homes containing more than 475 small balconies. The bronze, equestrian statue of King Philip III that stands in the cobblestone plaza provides a convenient rendezvous point for young Madrileños, and is an object of irreverent humor. They joke about meeting under *los huevos del caballo*, the eggs of the horse.

The area around Plaza Mayor is renowned for its rustic, subterranean taverns, called *mesones*, or *cuevas*, caves. Student minstrels dressed in traditional costumes often wander between *mesones* such as La Tortilla, La Guitarra and Las Cuevas de Luis Candelas. The last is named after an eighteenth-century rogue-about-town, whose last words before dancing on the gallows reportedly were "Be happy, my beloved city." Judging from the sangria-enhanced gaiety at Luis Candelas, it appears generations of Madrileños have slavishly heeded his words.

In centuries past, royalty and other noted personages stole through the dark streets for secret trysts at dimly lit taverns. According to legend, Goya met the business end of his lover's jealous husband's dagger outside a *meson*. Madrid's movers and shakers, including the royal family, still frequent Old Madrid.

Our dinner took place uptown in the modern Madrid of sleek office towers and fashionable shops. A pricey dinner and cabaret show at the upscale Melia Castilla Hotel drew Madrid's stylishly affluent, who exited their BMWs wearing Armani and fur. The show featured a Las Vegas-style revue with an Iberian twist: a flamenco number slipped into the American pop line up.

With midnight fast approaching, we schemed about how to spend the following hours. We could dance the night away – the newspaper, *El País*, listed nearly a hundred clubs and discos open after 3 a.m. – or we could venture to another bar. We also had our choice of jazz, salsa or even karaoke. But with our taste for flamenco tantalizingly whetted, we opted for Faraloe's, one of several clubs in Madrid dedicated to Andalucía's fiery music. Unfortunately, Faraloe's was virtually empty when we arrived. I thought we'd made a mistake. Perhaps we had come on the wrong night.

We were merely early.

We ordered drinks and a few more *tapas*, and soon the club began to fill. I was delighted to see that the audience would be almost exclusively Spanish, since I had heard that flamenco clubs in Madrid primarily cater to tourists, with shows long on slick commercialism and short on gritty Andalucían soul. But Madrid is a city of immigrants, from other parts of Spain; they cleave to romantic reminders of home.

Prior to the show, the audience indulged in a bit of do-it-yourself flamenco. They jammed the club's small stage to dance daring *sevillanas*. The official show began at 1 a.m. As flamenco purists will tell you, the guitar playing and the dancing, as artistic and exciting as they are, are subordinate to the singing. For it is the singing that most powerfully expresses the travails of the Gypsies, in whose culture flamenco is rooted.

The music and dancing brought shouts of appreciation from the audience, but the singing held center stage. The singer, a wiry man with angular features and wavy black hair, strained his voice into tortured, attenuated notes, cries of pain. His passion overwhelmed the audience; his every vocal nuance twisted it into ever tighter knots of raw emotion. A stunning performance; the audience exulted when he was through.

The strains of flamenco followed us out the door. We late-night novices had acquitted ourselves respectably, but fatigue overtook us before we could achieve the traditional end to a Madrid night: eating *churros* (fried doughnut strips) dunked in hot chocolate at dawn at the classic Chocolatería de San Ginés near Plaza Mayor.

Our taxi sped along Madrid's main boulevard. The lights that had shone on the sculpture of Cibeles and her lion-borne chariot in the eponymous plaza were now dark. By 5 a.m. the crowds had thinned to sparse clumps of pedestrians and freely flowing traffic.

But as the cab turned onto Plaza de las Cortes, I saw a sight that for me embodied the sweet joy of this nocturnal city. A man in a tuxedo and a woman in an evening dress suddenly emerged from the Palace Hotel. Arm in arm, engaged in easy conversation, they swung down the street toward Old Madrid. I could see chocolate-soaked *churros* in their future.

LISA JOHNSON IS THE EDITOR OF
THIS ANTHOLOGY. HER WORK HAS ALSO
APPEARED IN *PLAYGIRL*, *FIT
PREGNANCY* AND *MOTHERING* MAGAZINES.

MIGHT AS WELL TAKE IT

LISA JOHNSON

They were coming. I could hear the clicking of their boots, the slam of glass doors getting louder and louder. "*Ihre Passes, bitte.*" Two men entered. "Passports, please."

Lifting my T-shirt, I unzipped the money belt and handed them over.

The taller officer flipped mine open. "Lisa?"

I nodded.

He pressed his lips together and moved on to Tony, who had one of the newer passports with a silver star sticker at the bottom corner of the photo. Tony was convinced that everyone would think he was a government agent or something special because of it. Never mind that the picture itself confirmed another stupid American: irreverent grin and half-closed eyes hidden beneath a mop of curls.

"Do you have any drugs?"

It was September. We still had three days left on the Eurail passes, which were due to expire the following weekend. The farthest place we could think to go was Amsterdam.

Tony had been wooing me for two months when I casually mentioned the possibility of the two of us moving to Hungary for a year to teach English. I'd been guaranteed a job in a town famous for its wine festivals, and ever since my first taste of European travel, I'd missed the sense of freedom I'd

AMSTERDAM

experienced on the trains in Europe. The most excitement that my job at that time offered was deciding where to eat, and everyone on the commuter trains read nothing but newspapers. I needed a change.

Never believing he'd actually say yes, I was amazed when Tony quit his band on the verge of a record deal. Three days before we left, however, he announced he had no money. "Who do you think paid for all those flowers and fancy hotel rooms?" he'd snapped. At that point, it was too late. We'd had the going-away party.

"We'll make money there," he reassured me. Though I'd been saving for months, I convinced myself his argument was valid.

Everyone knows about Amsterdam: there are subtle signals everywhere that drugs are available *here*. Technically, you can smoke anywhere except on the streets. I walked around the famous canals while Tony partook of Dutch pleasures. Six hours later, it was time to head back.

"How much longer?" he repeated every half hour, like a child.

Why was I with him? I had already traveled the continent alone; he'd never been on a plane before our trip. I was an avid reader; he'd never even heard of Stephen King. Yet he was in love with me. And it had been a while.

Now, we couldn't afford to send him back.

"*Hauptbahnhof Passau!*" the station announcement tinkled in the silence.

"*Ihre Fahrkarten, bitte.*" Tickets. A conductor stamped our Eurail passes. "*Danke.*" I tucked them into the money belt under the band of my shorts as he left.

"We've been on this train forever," Tony said as he slapped the silver metal of the trash bin against the window repeatedly. "How many borders have we crossed?" You would think a twenty-six-year-old would have a longer attention span.

The past couple of weeks in Europe had been an adjustment, to put it mildly. I had to constantly figure out ways to entertain him. And somehow I had become responsible for buying him food. It was a real drag, this premature motherhood.

"Holland, Germany and Austria just now. And one more when we get back to Hungary," I replied. I kept trying to remind myself that this was his first overseas trip.

"Do you have any drugs?" the officer repeated.

"Me?" Tony scowled and turned to the window. "Of course not!"

"The bag please."

Tony shoved the daypack toward the officer, who unzipped the front pocket, rifled through the guidebook and touched the camera. He looked at his partner briefly, who lowered his eyebrows. "*Das andere jetzt.*" The other one now. He pointed at my backpack overhead. In all my months of traveling, I had never been searched.

There were two zippered pockets in front but the officer began by opening the buckle of the main compartment. He began taking out items individually: a jar of Nutella; a box of tampons; my contact lens case. He untwisted caps, pushed his fingers into pockets. Within moments, my journal, postcards and a sweatshirt were piled on the dirty green seat.

Tony sat across from me, hands tucked between his thighs. The inspector ignored us both and began to unzip the first pocket, removing Tony's wallet and scrutinizing his driver's license. Tony stared straight ahead, teeth touching repeatedly behind closed lips.

Exchanging looks with his partner in the doorway, the officer moved his fingers to the zipper on the second pocket, as Tony's face stiffened. His index fingers bent and pushed against each other.

Just then, a man's voice called in German from down the aisle. With the second pocket half open, the inspector tossed the wallet onto the seat and left without a word. The bag slowly rolled off the bench and onto the floor.

Tony's eyebrows knotted together. His lips were dry.

"What is wrong with you?"

"That was close." He let out a deep breath slowly, relaxing his face.

"What do you mean?"

"Remember that last café I went to?"

I sighed. "I lost count."

"Well, their stuff was really good, so I got a little extra."

"What do you mean *extra*?"

"Let me finish. I figured that since you can't get any in Hungary, I might as well take it with me." He smiled slowly, mouth still closed.

"You *what*?" An image of a police station flickered in my mind. "You have drugs on you?" I whispered.

"Shhhh!"

"You can't take stuff across the border!" I yelped, visions of swift deportation, my friends' faces at the airport.

"But nothing happened." He just sat there. "Hey, do we have any of that bread left?"

"I can't believe you!"

"What's the difference? We didn't get caught." He pulled the daypack toward him. "I wonder if the cheese is still good."

I yanked it back. "What do you mean, *we*? How could you drag me into this?" Who would I call from a foreign jail?

"Relax."

"Tony!" I fumed. "Do you have any idea what could have happened?

"You are just too uptight." He shook his head. "And to think I could have been famous. But no. I had to come with *you* instead."

The school year had barely started. "Look, you have to get rid of it."

"No!" he spat. "I spent my last twenty bucks on it! Besides, no one's checked."

"No one's checked? What do you call what just happened?"

"Well, they didn't find anything."

"We still have to get back to Hungary! Throw it out!"

"Where am I supposed to put it, Lisa?"

"In the toilet – I don't know!"

"Jeez." He got up, slamming his way out of the car. Moments later, his face reappeared at the window. "There aren't any toilets here."

"Follow the signs for the W.C." I pushed him back into the hallway.

How could I have been such an idiot? Why did I always end up stuck in relationships with jerks?

The train rocked on, passing through a dark tunnel, a village of brown and white cottages, the occasional child on a bicycle. European trains have the best windows. We passed mountains the color of bright green crayons, groves of thin trees in measured lines, hills of purple vineyards.

I tried to push aside the resentment, not knowing where my sense of duty came from. Was he now my responsibility because I had extended the invitation?

Tony reappeared after ten minutes, angrily flinging the backpack onto the overhead rack. We didn't speak.

Ten months to go.

We pulled into Sopron, the first station in Hungary. Heat rose from the dirt road; the sun shimmered desperately off the glass of a tiny restaurant. Around the ticket window was a cluster of old men. A girl in a faded dress kicked the dust along the tracks.

"Shit!" I heard an American's voice in the next compartment, and sounds of someone tapping the glass. "What do you think they did?"

From the nearest exit, two guys in handcuffs were being led off the train. The blond's head was lowered; I couldn't see the other's expression. They looked like us: cut-off Levi's; overstuffed, bumped-around backpacks; young.

"*Diese Richtung, bitte,*" a policeman said as he walked behind them, one hand lightly grasping each shoulder. Another toted their packs. They disappeared into the station as we slowly rolled off.

I looked at Tony. He stared out the window.

"What a waste," he said. "I could'a gotten away with it."

HELEN ELLIS IS A PERPETUAL TRAV-
ELER AND FORMER ANTIQUES DEALER.
SHE HAS TRAVELED TO THE UNITED
KINGDOM, SOUTH-EAST ASIA, CHINA
AND A NUMBER OF PACIFIC ISLANDS,
BUT HER TRUE LOVE HAS ALWAYS BEEN
GREECE.

PAROS

HELEN ELLIS

On the spur of the moment, having inadvertently gone to Piraeus (Athens' port) on a day when the ferry I wanted to catch didn't run, I hopped on a high-speed ferry for the Cyclades island of Paros. I was feeling a bit low, as my traveling companion had just flown back home to attend a funeral. It was 5 p.m. and the three-and-a-half-hour run took me from a gray early evening into a gathering darkness accentuated by increasingly ominous cloud formations. By the time we backed into the quay at Parikia, the port of Paros, it was as black as pitch and raining steadily; and there was I with no raincoat and nowhere to sleep for the night.

I had been to Paros briefly years before but didn't remember much; and I also knew that, in the way of the touristy islands of Greece, things would have changed. As I struggled off the ferry lugging my bits and pieces and trying to see through rainspotted specs, I was mentally berating myself. Depressed and disoriented, I decided to head for the nearest taverna and fish out my guidebook. As I was standing there with happy travelers milling all around, a voice said at my elbow, "Looking for a room, lady?" I turned and saw a small, sun-wizened man. "Lovely rooms, bath, all complete," he went on waving a pamphlet under my nose. I usually didn't take any notice of the *domatia* touts who met the ferries in the off-season, but this time all I wanted was a bed for the night

GREECE

and a chance to pull myself together and sort myself out; so I said okay.

His name was Stratos and he was ecstatic because it was the first rainfall on Paros for months. He loaded me into his little van, which is always a sure sign that the domatia (room) is out of town, swung my luggage into the back, and we were off. He had snared a French couple as well. He gave us a running commentary of the delights of Parikia as we whizzed past them and, sure enough, we were well out of town before he pulled into Stratos Studios. "Oh well," I thought, "I can change tomorrow." The room turned out to be very pleasant, whitewashed and airy, highlighted with Greek blue, and with the mod cons all in working order. I was so tired I put myself straight to bed, listening to the rain pattering on the roof and the sea whispering somewhere below.

Next morning I woke to sunshine. I found, to my delight, that I had a little balcony; and flinging the doors wide, I was astonished to see I had a view to die for! High on a headland, Stratos Studios overlooked the whole of the bay, from the sawtoothed rocks piercing a millpond sea (those which claimed a ferry two years ago) all the way to the port on my right. Stunted pine trees below hid glimpses of a rocky foreshore and little white cube houses scattered over the hillside. The whole thing was just so beautiful I was struck dumb with the realization that for once I had fallen on my feet.

I hastened to dress and went down to find Stratos to tell him I would stay. He was in the little breakfast room with his fishing nets stretched between two chairs. "*Kalimera*, lady," he greeted me with a big grin that said *I told you so*. He told me he was a fisherman and was getting ready for the winter when he shut the studios and went back to the age-old occupation of the islanders. I asked him about the shipwreck of the ferry.

"Terrible, terrible," he said. "Many lives lost. I saw it happening. I rang the port and said, 'That ferry's going to hit,' and then I ran to my boat and put out. I saved many lives that night. Very bad storm."

Later, as I sat on my balcony watching ferries scoot in and out, I could imagine it. The really weird part was that as I sat, the sky darkened and the light faded. It was as though I was settling in to watch a movie and the houselights were dimming. Huge storm clouds raced overhead and it grew so black that pinpoints of light came on all over the town. Then it rained, like no other rain; sweeping in across from Syros, horizontal, with a gale-force wind so thick that the whole scene just disappeared off the screen. For half an hour it raged, then suddenly it was gone. I thought, "Well, if it had been like that on the night of the ferry disaster, I wouldn't have seen the rocks either," but then . . .

Later I went into town. Everyone was sweeping the water from their shops. But they were smiling. Lovely rain, good for Paros, they said.

KAREN LEHMANN IS A POET AND FREE-
LANCE COPYWRITER LIVING IN
DENVER, COLORADO. AFTER GRADUAT-
ING FROM BARD COLLEGE, SHE
TRAVELED TO EUROPE AND ENDED UP
STAYING SIX YEARS.

BALKAN FRAGMENTS: GYPSY

KAREN LEHMANN

Doves coo. I am in the courtyard at Bosanska Street, number fifty-one. A two-room plaster house, crumbling. No plumbing. A garden and an outhouse out the back. Zemun. In this town we are all Gypsies. The town where storks nest on roofs, where fish jump from the Danube straight to the frying pan. The town was once on the Austro-Hungarian frontier, then after World War II it was repopulated with refugees from Hitler, Serb escapees from the Croatian Ustache, and returnees from the camps. All called back to Belgrade by Tito – the one-legged wonder, the man who could create a nightmare and make it seem a dream.

The Gypsies were placed in high-rises, newly built in the best concrete-silo communist architecture. Orthodox Serbs from Bosnia crawled to the cobblestone streets, setting their sacks down in the tiny houses left by the Austrian army three wars back. We have all been placed here, left to inhabit these houses, houses singing with ghosts. Houses built on bones. We add our bones to the pile and call it home. The slaves from Macedonia go to Makedonska Street to settle in, to raise their mixed blood children in this town on the outskirts of the city, far from the olive groves, far from their bastard Greek fathers.

But the Gypsies are most unhappy. From the camps they came – starved, beaten, hardly noticed – and were stuffed into

YUGOSLAVIA

small rooms high above the ground. Rumors flew: men were not made to live so high; those who didn't jump would be transformed into monkeys. Was it some misplaced communist charity that deemed the new high-rises the perfect place for Gypsy hearts? Did the partisan general intend special reparation, or was the vision to rehabilitate? Maybe the politicians really believed the modernity of the towers could reconstruct the old ways, reform the dirty Gypsy bands, amend their wanderings, make good party members of them.

I am often told to beware of these *tsigani* with their dusky skin, their lice, their men with those unfathomable brown eyes. A Gypsy man looks at me and sees right through to the flower, and I am wet unwillingly, wet and wanting there on the bus. I return his stare through thick glass, glass designed to protect.

Late at night. Drunk, I stagger out to the yard to pee; can't bear the stench of the dark outhouse. I crouch, listening to the Gypsy distance. Out of the high-rises they run on dirty common land; an acre of mud between towers and the bus stop. The Gypsies light illegal fires, feast and wail, sing and couple there. I try to rise, and stumble, curse, and regain my balance. For some minutes I stand, aware of the moon, and listen to the distant music, the beat of drum and tambourine. Oh yes, cliché I guess, but true, too true here, true so far, so far away from . . . I am drunk, and unwilling to admit misery. In my heart, I hold the coyote moans of Gypsy souls, of Gypsy ghosts, their fire and their tambourines contain as much of me as can be.

Dirty – ten days without a bath in this house with no plumbing. Ten days too cold to squat in the courtyard while Mama K. dumps buckets of water over my bikinied body. Too anxious to ask the neighbors again for a shower, to request the water heater turned on again. Too expensive. Ten days dirty as a Gypsy here in this too-quaint Eastern European village, the backwater of Belgrade. Drunk is good. Drunk and dirty, pissing in the yard, wailing with the Gypsy boys. *Oh what, oh what would Father think? What would my friends from Liberal Arts say? Daddy, do you know the miles traveled to this spot, this Boris and Natasha trap – the loving husband brutal now; the language I can't comprehend?* What I

wanted, what I thought, my bubbly dreams of European artistry –
gone. The miles that have led me to this leftover refugee town – the
cobbled streets, the whitewashed walls. Drunk, yes. A Gypsy
finally, after all the education, the rooms and rugs, the music
lessons. Ten days without a bath, drunk with Gypsy fire, I sway,
and cleanse myself with wishing.

JENNIFER SPIEGEL IS CURRENTLY A
MASTER OF FINE ARTS CANDIDATE IN
FICTION AT ARIZONA STATE
UNIVERSITY. SINCE THE EVENTS IN
"WALTER" TOOK PLACE, SHE HAS BEEN
TO CHINA AND SOUTH AFRICA. THIS
PIECE WAS FIRST PUBLISHED IN "YOU
ARE HERE."

WALTER
JENNIFER SPIEGEL

The Berlin Wall had come down and Gorbachev was still in power.
Madonna posters adorned Helsinki. Iraq was on the verge of attack-
ing Kuwait. I was a kid, a college girl; my hair was a different
shade of red. Some called it "bozo orange." I preferred to think of
it as brassy or sun-drenched.

The snapshots of that summer are dusty and dated. Already they
have the pallor of rerun TV: nostalgic, sweet and a little sad.

Man and Woman in Red Square, Moscow (July 1990)
Walter is in his early thirties, so he's old. We're on a five-week
Russian language excursion. He's Canadian and possibly a man-
agement professor at Harvard – I think that's what he said.

Once he told everyone, "I'm not going to pretend we'll keep in
touch." Then he had looked at us, including the girl he was having
a fling with. "We won't. So don't write me."

The fling girl is older than me, cute and flirtatious. On
Nevsky prospekt, in St. Petersburg, she shared an ice-cream
cone that dripped from both ends with this guy in our program. Watching Walter, I found it seductive, titillating.

At the Kremlin, Walter and I stand alone. The Twenty-
Eighth Communist Party Congress is about to begin. Dan
Rather is somewhere around. During the past month, we've
been to the Bolshoi Ballet and the Moscow McDonald's.

RUSSIA

I've attended the circus with my teacher, gone to Peter the Great's glamor-pad palace on the outskirts of town. I've eaten a hair ball baked into my breakfast.

Pushkin, Gogol and Chekhov whisper constantly in our ears. The Soviet Union hovers on the cusp of something momentous: everyone's talking about *glasnost*, *perestroika* and that revolutionary, madcap man Boris Yeltsin.

Our Russian is hideous.

In the middle of Red Square, Walter – *Wall Street Journal* tucked under arm – says to me, an unglamorous girl with a hot pink fanny pack around her waist, "Out of all the people on this trip, you're the one I'd like to know what happens to." Grammatically awkward, utterly unprecedented.

His comment is devoid of sexual intrigue, ulterior motive or monetary possibility. And that's why it hits me hard, like the storming of my own winter palace.

Two Women Sipping Cappuccino at an Outdoor Café, Venice (July 1990)

It's her summer. I envisioned gondolas and poetry, hand-holding and fresh flowers. I got Siobhan. We sit together in Piazza San Marco, the pigeons having disappeared when the moon flushed the sky.

I will trash the pink fanny pack.

I will experience Michelangelo and the Sistine Chapel like an afterglow.

I will work out till the marzipan and Nutella leave minimal traces on my hips.

I won't buy the next album by the Cure.

I'll even stop studying Russian.

But I won't drop Siobhan.

Someday, I will ask for her memories. She will speak about the two of us hunting for sanitary napkins around the Charles Bridge in Prague, communicating with strangers in a peculiar pantomime. She'll recall four people in a three-man tent camping near Berlin Wall remains – the rain pouring down, seeping into the sides. She'll note artichoke pizza outside Vatican City; pizza is always *so* important. She'll talk about a Venice walk under a full moon with her boyfriend, when they knew they'd never marry but loved each other anyway. She'll remember an all-night train out of Zagreb – sleeping on her feet and breathing through an open window while moaning aloud.

Someday, I will tell her about popping blisters on toes with sterile syringes. I'll share a gloomy, bittersweet stroll through the Jewish Cemetery in Prague. I'll talk about the Saint Sebastian paintings, a vaporetto in Venice, tears outside Salzburg cathedrals.

Later, when we speak, both of us will remember Piazza San Marco and cappuccino. We will evoke the image of two women sitting together under Italian stars, alone and wistful, staring into each other's eyes, understanding what would be.

Though my snapshots yellow and the men are memories, Siobhan is still a sister, a song I know well.

There have been college degrees in unrelated fields. I've abandoned careers and towns. Intellectual snobbery is a fashion accessory I've worn to parties.

My passport is stunning, stamped and suggestive. Drag shows in Harlem, dinners at the Waldorf Astoria, nights on dung floors in Africa, babies held in Shanghai orphanages, and walks through ruins in Rome have punctuated stiff days. I've worked at Disneyland and Amnesty International, where I stole Harrison Ford's address from the PR person's Rolodex. Once, I thought I had breast cancer. Another time, I prayed for divine intervention. A man exposed himself to me in Central Park. I followed an elephant through the Swazi bush. For a while, I didn't wear makeup. I've lived alone in Manhattan and crawled home to my parents in Phoenix. There's been a coma. A lot's been said.

But this is what I'm thinking: *Walter, where are you now?*

Walter, in your knee-high yellow socks and dark blue shorts – a man's purse straight out of "Seinfeld" in your hands – what has become of you? Have you headed into middle age with thinning hair and wrinkled skin, the Prufrock of my European vacation?

And would you recognize me today? Would you know who I am? Did you know I now fret about skin damage and the lines around my mouth?

I like to picture us in Antwerp or Bruges. In Belgium, we'd drink beer with a trace of something raspberry; we'd eat cheese dipped in mustard. You'd show me pictures of your kids; I'd tell you about the books I've read.

"Walter," I'd say, "talk to me. Tell me things."

Though so much has happened in the past decade, all I can think about is what hasn't been. And that is what I'd talk about, boring you with details.

What would you say?

If we met today, in Portugal or Beijing, in New Delhi or San Salvador, would I have to do all the talking?

Would you throw your eyes over me as if I were naked and needed to be covered; when you saw time elapsed on my face, scars on my body hinting at disaster, stories on paper coming out of a swollen leather bag. When you saw these things, after so many years, would you be disappointed?

My long-gone Walter.

Are you disappointed?

AVIYA KUSHNER WORKED IN
JERUSALEM FOR A YEAR AS A TRAVEL
WRITER FOR THE *INTERNATIONAL
JERUSALEM POST*. SHE IS CURRENTLY
A TEACHING FELLOW IN THE MASTER
OF FINE ARTS PROGRAM AT THE
UNIVERSITY OF IOWA.

AFTER A MONTH IN GERMANY
AVIYA KUSHNER

A recipe for red cabbage arrives in the mail, along with a note: "I hope you don't think we are monsters." The recipe is from Gerti, a blond girl from Munich's suburbs who's studying to be a geography teacher. She's also the only person I met during a month in Germany who admitted that her father was a Nazi.

I talked with many twentysomething Germans who had given great thought to questions relating to the Holocaust, guilt, memory and reparation. There was an incredible interest in all things Jewish in modern Germany, including Hebrew language and literature, and even klezmer music. Travel to Israel was also popular, with at least four flights leaving Munich for Tel Aviv on a typical summer morning, usually sold out.

Of course, few Jews live in Germany. Today, more Jews than at any time since the war – about 100,000 – call Germany home, but these are a smidgen of the eighty-two million citizens in the country. The fascination is with the nonexistent, the dead millions who sometimes seem to define the present for this nation.

The Germans I met who were around my age – twenty-four that summer – all had to live their lives with the stigma of being "German." Flashing a passport often brought a scowl, they told me. A few said they were also deeply and personally embarrassed. A gay man confided that the Nazi record on

GERMANY

178

homosexuality haunted him. He knew that, like my entire family, had he been alive then, he might not have survived.

I went to Germany on the tab of the German government. The Germans paid for food, hotels and transportation, and our group of young Americans was treated like honored guests. Odd, I must admit, to sit at the Munich City Council, when a mere sixty years ago the place was – well, we know what it was.

That sense of unmentionability kept coming up. A tour guide hired by the German government to show us the city passed a building and said: "This was the Gestapo building, where the Nazis took the Jews and questioned them and tortured them and so on and so forth." *And so on and so forth.* No one actually said "and slaughtered and gassed and choked and beat and burned."

What to say and what not to say often comes down to the silent space of sculpture, of stone memorials to the dead. Berlin has large plaques with the names of death camps at its subway entrances, which are both obvious and powerful. But Munich has precious little. The world's third-largest synagogue is now a department store, with a small plaque commemorating what it once was, placed five hundred feet away. The plaque is written in German. Those who know know, and that's it.

A major hotel in Berlin, however, keeps the name of the Jewish family that once owned it. Then, as now, it remains the ritziest hotel in the city. The story is different in every city, family and individual's mouth.

I volunteered to come to Germany. I wrote an essay, asked my professors for recommendations, endured the inevitable questioning from friends and family on why I would want to go *there*. I was curious, and wanted to see what Germany was, and is.

To be in Berlin's Tiergarten and note that each tree is numbered in yellow, the Holocaust takes on a new meaning. What is Nazi, and what is German, and what is human?

Germany confuses. It is green and deep, beautiful and cold, even in July. It is wealthy. The people are tall, the women often grazing six feet. Shoes come in big sizes; beer in the famous, generous doses. All that is Jewish is not here, and yet Yiddish is half

German. And my grandfather learned Talmud in German, the way I learned midrash in English.

Germany was once the center of the Jewish world. I could not forget this as I traveled from Munich to Gauting, to Hamburg, to Frankfurt, to Berlin. So much of who I am comes from these great forests, the long railroad tracks, the heavy seas of northern Germany. This I have in common with Gerti: our tie to the land is like our tie to cooking, our love of food, our sustenance. And yet she knows who her family was; it is I who must imagine, who must fill in the holes all my life with dreams, nightmares and travel.

LORNA SMEDMAN TRAVELED SOME OF
THE BAMBOO HUT AND GEKKO ROUTES
THROUGH SOUTH ASIA IN 1999 AND
2000. SHE IS COMPLETING A
COLLECTION OF SHORT STORIES
TITLED *MOSS* AND RUMINATING ABOUT
BEING A FIRST-TIME PROPERTY
OWNER IN *MAKING HOUSE*.

PINK DRESS

LORNA SMEDMAN

For Kim Lyons

On the train to Florence, she met a Spanish woman named Isabelle who told her that they wouldn't rent a hotel room to a single woman. Would she like to share? That was fine; Italy was the only place where she could afford to stay in a hotel instead of a youth hostel.

They went to a large, dark stone pensione on Via Cerrentani. The outside was covered in scaffolding. It was run by two old women – she presumed they were sisters – both wearing ankle-length black dresses. One led them through a labyrinth of halls, up short then long flights of stairs, and down many shiny dark corridors, a ring with dozens of ancient intricately toothed keys jouncing against her hip, until they came to a tiny door. Even she, who was fairly short, would have to duck a little to get inside, and Isabelle was tall. They looked at each other in disbelief as the old woman rattled one of her keys in the lock. On the other side of the tiny door was an enormous high-ceilinged room filled with many beds, several imposing wardrobes, a sturdy wooden table with six chairs, and an overstuffed couch.

"*Letto matrimoniale*," roared the proprietess, shaking the footboard of one double bed. "*Uno, due, tre*." There were three double beds in the room and one single. The wallpaper had enormous gray feathers floating across a greenish mauve

FLORENCE

background. Each must have been about four feet long and exquisitely detailed. Quaint French doors opened out onto a small balcony overlooking a tiny courtyard with emerald green grass and a brilliant white, carved birdbath at its center.

It was her first visit to Florence and she did not spend much time in that wonderful room. She did not spend any time with Isabelle, who, on her first day, struck up an acquaintance with one of the young men selling prints on the Ponte Vecchio. As far as she could tell – for Isabelle didn't speak much English, and she no Spanish – Isabelle spent her days in Florence hanging out with this guy. She wasn't in love with him and, as far as she could discern, they weren't having sex. Isabelle had introduced her to him the first time she walked across that bridge, and after that when she passed, they were always deep in conversation, though Isabelle did not speak any Italian either.

She, on the other hand, went everywhere – to every church, museum, plaza and garden. She crossed every bridge that spanned the milky turquoise Arno; hiked up the hot hills to Fiesole; bought bread, cheese and fruit for lunch; and splashed her face in fountains. One afternoon, she fell asleep in the shade of a hedge in the Boboli Gardens. She sat in cafés and read books like Vasari's *Lives of the Painters, Sculptors and Architects* and Dante's *Vita Nuova*, and bought many postcards. She nearly wept over several paintings. Several times, she returned for dinner to the same small *trattoria* where the owner had taken her arm on the first night and steered her back into the kitchen, then pointed to a place at a long bench on one side of a big table filled with noisy men, women and children, old and young. They were his family, she guessed, and she ate whatever was passed around communally.

Even when she came back twice, then a third time, no one in the family paid any attention to her, except the old grandma, who sometimes leaned over and patted her arm.

Buongiorno. Grazie. Mi scusi. Buonasera. This was the extent of her Italian, and these words would delineate the depth and breadth of her interactions with the people of Florence during those ten days.

She had never felt so invisible. At first it was a relief, after three months of traveling and constantly being the center of attention, the object of hospitality. It had been three months of trading the same basic personal facts, discussing for hours the differences of culture, and struggling to find enough common language. Sometimes, silence was an utter blessing.

Steering clear of other tourists, she encountered a table of loud Americans one evening at a restaurant. They were arguing with the waiter over a basket of bread that had never arrived; they didn't want to pay the extra charge that had been added to their bill. The waiter smiled, studied the check and shrugged his shoulders. What could he do? "It is the principle of the thing," one of the customers explained angrily to his friends. "Why pay for a basket of bread that never came?"

"*Pane*, see? Here on the bill? Look!" The American's arm swept the remains of the tabletop as he looked up at the waiter. "No *pane*. *Capisci?* No *pane*, no pay."

Finally the waiter gave up. They wanted *pane*? No, they were finished. The waiter turned his back, stomped into the kitchen, and returned with a huge basket of bread chunks under his arm.

"*Pane?*" he yelled, "*Pane?*", and started throwing the bread at the Americans. Behind him, two other men were similarly armed, and the Americans jumped up and ran out, the three men in close pursuit hurling bread chunks.

On the fifth day, the other sister woke them early with loud knocking on their tiny door, and made it understood that they had to change rooms. She led them through more hallways, up and down other staircases, and stopped at an enormous set of double doors. She and Isabelle sputtered with laughter at the sight of these, trying to imagine what colossal suite awaited them on the other side. When the doors opened, however, they were met with a room barely as wide as the doorway, one that only just fitted a double bed, a small dresser and a washbasin. The sister again shook the footboard on the bed, shouting, "*Letto matrimoniale!*" Then she counted, pointing from one woman to the other, "*Uno, due.*" She pointed again to the bed, as if trying to assist them in sleeping arrangements.

They parted for the day, Isabelle sad that it would be her last visit with her friend on the Ponte Vecchio. She wandered out for an espresso. After having spent the previous day wandering around, thinking about Savonarola, this day she spent fantasizing: she was a thirteenth-century Finnish nun who had escaped from a nunnery and after much hardship had found her way to Florence in pursuit of the poet Dante. There were probably no nunneries in Finland, not then and maybe not now, but yes, she was from a remote area bordering Russia, where in fact there was an Orthodox Russian nunnery. Here her family had sent her, not entirely against her will, as she was of a studious nature. Literacy would turn out to be much more profound than she ever could have dreamed, for there was an old Italian priest who, through a series of misadventures, became attached to her church. He taught her to read the language of his country, and finally, on his deathbed, gave her some poems from a man named Dante Alighieri. After reading them by candlelight that night, she knew then that there was a conversation she and Dante were destined to have, and so she made her escape. And now here she was, suffering from the heat of this climate, shy and strange, closely observing and imitating the people of this city in order to get by. She discovered the poet's quarters, persuaded a servant to give her entry, but the man was not at home. She wandered about the neighborhood, several times starting because she could sense his closeness. And then impulse directed her to a steep wooden staircase inside a small shop. She went down it and caught a glimpse of him – the swirling edge of his short felt cape, dark leather underneath; the neat queue of hair under the brim of his hat – as he swiftly rounded the turn in the stair. She clattered down faster, but it was too late. The sun outside blinded. He was gone. Tears filled her eyes.

She went back to the room early. Isabelle was there, lying on the *letto matrimoniale*, reading a Spanish magazine. They went back outside to get gelato, their new room hot and stuffy.

The one narrow window opened onto the scaffolding on the main face of the pensione. When they returned she washed her underwear and pink dress in the little sink near the window, and figured out how to string the clothesline from her backpack across it. Isabelle was very amused that she traveled with rope.

It was hard to sleep because it was so hot. Isabelle soon got out of bed and shed her T-shirt and underwear; she followed suit.

When she woke up in the morning, Isabelle was lying with her long limbs sprawled wildly, the sheet trampled to the end of the bed. She had been squished to the very edge of the *letto matrimoniale*. It was already hot. Isabelle's skin gave off a slight shimmer of sweat. A redhead with very pale skin, her entire body was covered with freckles. She propped her head up and tried to decide if she thought Isabelle was attractive or not.

The freckles all over were a bit of a surprise. There was a wonderful curve to her waist, but Isabelle's nipples were big and puffy and very pink, as if stung.

Suddenly, her eyes felt like they were twitching. She leaned forward. There were ants, dozens of them, crawling across Isabelle's body: reddish brown ants, the same color as freckles and just as small. If she blurred her vision a little, it looked as though the freckles were shifting and undulating all over the surface of Isabelle's skin. She glanced around the sheets; there were no ants on her side. Perhaps the ants were too small to tickle, so slight that Isabelle couldn't sense them. Maybe their tiny legs were refreshing, brushing against her hot skin like little breezes or feathers.

She heard a gritty, shuffling sound and looked over her shoulder. There were four pairs of dusty boots lined up on the scaffolding platform outside the window; above the boots, four pairs of overalled legs. Her pink dress hung limply on its line; there were bars on the windows, but no curtains to draw. Gently she shook the pale, freckled shoulder of Isabelle, then less gently, and shushed her when she peevishly began to protest. Pointing to the window with her finger to her lips, it took a few seconds for Isabelle to figure out what so many boots were doing there. Then she pointed to Isabelle's belly, where the ants continued their busy sojourn. Hitting Isabelle with the pillow a few times to help get them off, she began laughing. Isabelle was not amused and began to pack up her things. They settled the money for the room and said goodbye quietly, self-conscious with the workmen standing just outside their room.

She then went out and successfully located the shower in the labyrinth of halls. She had been planning to wear the pink dress that day, so she could wash out her two T-shirts. The dress was still damp. She had bought it in Paris – a thin, short, jersey dress with a rather plunging V neck and little cap sleeves. It was fun to wear in Paris, but now she wasn't sure that it was quite the thing that an escaped Finnish nun should wear. Nothing else was clean, however.

Soon after she had returned to the room, there was a loud banging at the door. It was the sisters – both of them. "*E meglio che te ne vada*," they said in unison, flinging their thumbs over their shoulders. Her phrases didn't get her far in persuading them to let her stay, even one more night. "*Vattene*." The thumbs jerked impatiently. Even if she had been able to speak Italian, she would certainly never get the old women to believe that she had once been a nun, and was still pure of heart and a true friend of the great poet Dante Alighieri. That underneath her pink dress – contrary to what half a dozen Florentine workmen might think they knew – she was completely invisible, innocent as marble.

BRENT OLSON SPENDS MOST OF HIS
TIME LIVING AND WRITING IN
COLORADO.

THE OTHER SHORE

BRENT OLSON

Waves track the passing time. I sit on one of the rocks on the shore
and let my feet hang just above the water, counting the waves while
I wait to make phone calls. Just above me, up by the road, a phone
booth stands absurdly alone in the middle of a brick sidewalk. Cars
pick up speed on their way along the Italian coastline and barely
notice the small path leading over the railroad tracks and down the
embankment to the rocky coast of the Mediterranean Sea. The clat-
ter of Riviera resort hotels stops before this stretch of shore, so it
provides a nice place to sit, rest and pay attention to different noises.

It's lonely this far out of town. San Remo is two miles away.
The phone booth is isolated; the waves come in slower, further
apart; the trains are louder; the rocks more rugged. The noises this
far away from the city erode a person, remind them of time.

I have developed a ritual. If someone else is using the phone, I
climb down to the coast and count two hundred waves before
checking to see if they are done. I wait seventy-five waves if
the phone at Mom's is busy and one hundred and twenty-five
every time I call Amanda and hear that the Telecom Italia
mobile customer I am trying to reach is unavailable. Each
wave rolls in from right to left and only counts if it reaches
the bottom of my feet.

This morning someone is using the phone. The waves are
cold against the bottom of my bare feet and it chills the rest

ITALY

of me despite the surprising warmth of the autumn air. A train rumbles past, cutting off the light from the street above. Forty-four waves crumble while it shakes the hill and echoes in the tunnel further down the track. The waves slowly and deliberately lap at the rocks they have shaped for centuries.

It's easier to count waves at night than during the day. Beneath the sunshine, I have trouble remembering what number follows 112. It's too easy to look up at the horizon as it fades into the blue of the sky. It's too easy to lose track of the passing now and slip into the future or past tense. It's easy to slip away from here – the solid rock and cold water – and drift to there: the invisible somewhere possibly visible in the horizon. Easy to wonder if that horizon exists at all; how far away it is; what secrets it clutches.

Somewhere in that distance I lose myself and remember how alone I am. During the night, I think I can sense the other shore – all the life of it, its magic, its mystery – in the waves that roll over my feet. But during the day, I lose it in the horizon; it melts in the gray mush that separates the sea from the sky. I can't discern a future, a dream or any knowledge in that blending of air and water. How can you know the other shore? And how, in that ignorance, that distance, can you help but feel alone?

I sit on the bench in the sun and squint through its reflection as it bounces blue off the water. I sit with too many futures lost; too many dreams caught in the midst of a horizon; too many shores to ponder; too many reasons to feel alone. Inevitably, I lose count of the waves and turn periodically to watch the cars as they pass the phone booth, heading into the tunnel under the part of the mountain that slides into the sea.

I'd woken up early to call home. The line in Wisconsin was busy so I've decided to wait and count the waves. After twenty, I start to wonder if it's worth it. I know the conversation well enough, have had it before, undoubtedly will have it again. Mom asks the same questions and I give the same answers. Dad and I are still trying to figure out how to talk on the phone. After fifty-three waves I quit thinking about Wisconsin at all and start thinking about Taggia, the next town up the coast. Another forty-six cool, wet tickles under my feet convince me that Mom and Dad, landlocked in Wisconsin without a horizon that blurs, wouldn't say anything worthwhile. Careful thinking for three more waves convinces me that nothing I would say would be important or understood. Taggia grows large in my thought horizon, and after another glance over the water, I follow the cars into the tunnel and to Taggia.

I find the one gear that works on the rickety old yellow bike my boss has loaned me and ride through the tunnel, almost scraping my knuckles against the rock walls to avoid the speeding cars. A couple of miles later I roll into the ancient town built on a hill right above the sea. It has the same narrow streets, crooked windows, winding staircases, crumbling churches and hidden cafés that dominate the non-resort towns along the coast. I spend my day drifting through an antique market, stumbling through the underbrush inside an ancient Roman fort, and napping underneath an old fig tree. The people of the town seem older than those in the other towns along the Riviera, more worn, but they possess a quickness to smile or frown that belies a more pervasive patience. Within their smiles and winks there is a deep pause, a growing valley between unending waves.

In the afternoon, I sit down outside a café in the square with a gelato and a glass of orange juice. The café is empty except for the *barista* and a couple of teenagers playing pinball. By the town square, just outside the café, buses, blue and boxy, stop and turn off their engines. No one gets off and no one gets on. They restart their motors and drive around the large statue that dominates the square. A man – muscled and intent, carved out of bronze – stands chained to a rock while concrete waves, tipped in gold leaf, roll beneath him. I look closely at the wrinkles around his eyes, the pain and sadness in his mouth. Beneath his feet a plaque explains that the statue is dedicated to the partisans who died fighting the fascists in World War II. A pigeon perches on his shoulder, pecking at the bronze. Prometheus with a pigeon. I do what I always seem to do on afternoons in new towns – drink orange juice and write a horrible poem about tides and Prometheus and pigeons.

An old woman walks slowly to the table next to me. She sits down and smiles a gapped grin, her face rippled with wrinkles – the picture of an old Italian matriarch. Her eyes are set deep behind her forehead. They follow the birds and buses slowly. Her lips are thin and active. Her hands shake above the table while she drinks her cappuccino as if they had practiced their quakes for years before finding the correct pace, broken only by an unexpected calmness when she brushes her thick gray hair behind her ears.

She sits for a few minutes and I write another line, erase it, and write it again. Then she speaks. Her voice is quiet, as one would expect, but the sounds are clear, though I can barely understand the Italian. I apologize. "*Non parlo italiano.*" I don't speak Italian. We both chuckle and go back to our own worlds for a few minutes. I scribble more lines in my notebook, erase them, scribble them again, and count out syllables on the tips of my fingers.

She folds and refolds a piece of paper with names and phone numbers. Neither of us sits still for long. Neither of us can totally forget the other. Neither of us can totally forget ourselves, our aloneness.

When she speaks again I turn, attentive, determined to catch what I can of her Italian. She points at her hand and speaks quickly, but clearly. I smile when I think I should, frown other times, say "*si*" on cue, "hmm" and "ooh." Every now and then I shrug and look at her eyes, deep brown and buried in age. She, as far as I can gather, tells me about her medical problems. She asks me to feel her pulse – easy to find through her thin skin – and the bump in the middle of her hand, obscured by the wrinkles and hidden between the more obvious protrusions of knuckles and veins. She talks about how the doctors keep giving her the run-around and how her children don't understand. She talks faster and faster and my memory of Italian flees before her rush. She pauses for a second before she asks me a question. Again, I apologize, "*Non ho capito, non parlo italiano,*" but she keeps talking, keeps asking, explaining herself, begging me to feel her pulse again. She then asks what I do, and I tell her I teach children English. She asks if I'm German.

"*Non,*" I say, "*sono Americano. Parlo inglese e francese.*" She starts talking again. I say "*si*" when I think it's appropriate.

It's getting dark and I still have to ride home. The tunnel is dark enough during the day, and my knees still have scabs from a previous bike wreck. I point at my watch and tell her I have to go. I start to stand up but she is quicker than me. She reaches across the table, takes my hands one more time and holds them while looking into my eyes. I don't know what she sees there, but she thanks me. She thanks me for listening, for sitting with her, for understanding. We laugh again and I tell her I only understand a little. Between slow chuckles she tells me, "*No, hai capito.*" You understand.

"*Troppo poco.*" Too little.

She stands up next to me, very slowly, and looks me in the eye. With the practiced patience that seems prevalent throughout the town, she taps me three times on the chest, once with each word. "*Hai capito molto.*" She waves goodbye. "*Grazie.*"

How do we know the other shore? I never learned her name. We met for a moment on an October afternoon in Italy. She sat across from me with tumors hidden in the wrinkles of her hands, and eyes that had seen more waves than I could imagine. I think of that woman, now, when I think of the sea, when I think of the vast lone-liness that separates one shore from another. I think of her when I find myself closer to people than I expect to be, and more alone. I thought of her last week when my lover asked me, "Who are you? How do I know you? How do you know anyone?" I wanted her to feel the old woman's hands, to hear her voice and see the wrinkles around her eyes. I wanted her to feel the old woman tap her chest and tell her that she understood much. I wanted her to look into her eyes and try to understand, and in trying, maybe succeed. But I couldn't say anything, so we stayed quiet. In that silence her breath slowed to the rhythm of the sea and sleep. I closed my eyes in the dark and thought of the phone booth. I thought of the statue in the square and the old woman tapping my chest. I thought of loneliness and love. I thought of the other shore, so distant, yet so close, falling asleep next to me.

I ride home through the tunnel just as dusk falls over the sea. The grays of evening fade into blacks of night. After the tunnel I park the bike next to the road and take off my shoes. I start count-ing the waves. The tide is out and the sand is wet and cold between my toes. At the water's edge, the waves cool my feet further and their rolls rumble in my ears, giving resonance to the old woman's voice that still rings in my head. In my heels I can feel the echoes of the other shore, not quite so distant, not quite so alone.

Waves and echoes of waves. Forty-four waves for a train to pass. Twenty-eight remembered waves in the time it takes not to answer a question. One wave goodbye from a wrinkled, tumored hand. I go back to collect my bike, and walk barefoot along the road, pushing it next to me. I pass the phone booth. Tomorrow I'll call home.

saimen
(7 replies)

home sweet home . . . aaaaaaaaaarrrgggghhhhhhh

man, i just came back from a sixteen-month trip and i am totally lost. my neighbors don't greet me anymore (they used to do that every day!!! even their dogs ignore me now), well they almost forgot that i'm still a tenant of an apartment, or let's say a rat hole, in their house. hm. the man at the coffee shop isn't there anymore, sad . . . hey everybody looks so frustrated in the streetcar . . . come on, i thought, the world is not THAT BAD, sigh! any ideas how i can get over all this . . . (i know packing would be the best, but it isn't an option right now). give me some help!!! should i pretend being a traveler in my own country? now that would be definitely an experience . . . pfffffffff

Paul McCafferty
1.

RUN

Just run for the hills whenever you can and enjoy the small bits of freedom you find.

to live is human, to travel is life, to be at that fork in the road once more is where i want to be!

becca
2.

being home

Think of the few things that you would have liked to do while traveling, but couldn't because you didn't stay in one place long enough, and do those things. For me, it is taking language classes (also helps me feel like I'm doing something constructive to prepare for future travels), pursuing new hobbies (like rock climbing, photography), and reading some books I couldn't get while traveling (library access).

175%   Page:

Being home is also a good opportunity to renew flagging friendships; but this may not be something you want to do, depending on how different your lives and perspectives are becoming. I've drifted apart from many of my old friends, but with one certain group I've become better friends than ever since I've been back. Renewing these friendships has made it a lot more bearable to be working a regular job in that dull old native country again.

The advice about viewing home as just another travel destination is trite, but useful. Find out about hiking trails, oddball tourist attractions, historic sites, etc., in your own area and convince a friend or two to try something new with you. And remember your traveler mindset. Be adaptable, try not to be judgmental, and just look at the attitude of people you meet at home as you would those of people from yet another culture. Try to be amused rather than frustrated as you observe things you dislike or disagree with.

Kanada
3.

!

Open your doors to travelers in your town. That's what I always do when I get back from a long trip. It lets you stay part of the "community" per se and allows you to give back the good that has been given to you.

Besides that, volunteering while looking for a job is a great idea . . . you need to keep busy when you get back . . . if you don't, reverse culture shock is that much worse because depression from isolation and loneliness compounds the fact that you already feel like shit for not being able to move on any longer.

Hope that helps you a bit, or at least gives you some ideas.

– Gabriel Murray

<u>wildfruit</u>
4.

Yep

pretending to be a traveler in your own country is the only solution. it's what i've been doing, otherwise i go insane. i live in hostels and work with travelers so i still have that travel buzz and am surrounded by people that want that little bit more out of life. I grew up in london and have been traveling for ten years and every time i come back from abroad i live somewhere different. i've just come back from a year away and on saturday i'm moving to ireland for a while. so definitely become a traveler in your own country and take the world with a pinch of salt.

<u>Neonrickshaw</u>
5.

coming home sucks

you know you had a good time when you come home and are miserable . . .

so, you know how to put together a good trip: nice work!

Ready?

#1 get a job and WORK

#2 SAVE your money (daily budget like you had while on the road)

#3 TRAVEL!

that's it, work – save – travel

you'll be out there again very soon *compadre*.

Where2Next
6.

The People Cure

One of my cures when I am stuck at home is to keep up with letters and emails to people I met on the road, especially locals. As time goes on, you never know what those sort of contacts will lead to – future travel, overseas projects, political activism, etc. It's all too easy to let travel friendships slide, but then that just gives you one more thing to be depressed about. But developing these relationships allows you to think of your trip as the start of something, rather than an ending.

– James Wilbrot

Victoria
Martinez
7.

my cure

I got back six weeks ago (I'm still counting how long it's been since I've been back). The day I left I cried off and on in three airport terminals; reentering the U.S. is surreal (airports are surreal); then I got back to my apartment and got online.

I researched and researched; shunned my friends; went to work and came back home to the computer; and six weeks later, I have my cure: I'M GOING BACK.

I'm giving up everything I've got and I'm going to move there. In about five months. I feel happy again.

I recognize that after I've lived there for a year or two, I will need a new cure (coming back home?) but that's the way it goes.

AUTHOR'S ACKNOWLEDGMENTS

Thank you to so many friends for their excitement about this book, as well as the business advice and reassurance that it would really happen; to my family for the most perfect college graduation gift ever, and the courage to let me go; to the dynamic duo of Rodman and Rodman for loving and persistent legal assistance; to Janet Austin and the crew at Lonely Planet for their belief in the idea for this book and their willingness to carry it through; to all the contributing writers, including those whose work does not appear in this volume; to my sixth-grade teacher, Mr. Cable, whose assignment to write a well-researched travel journal got me aching to get to Europe in the first place; to Paj, a terrific husband, always ready to give me time to do my thing; and to my son, Izzy, the well of all my stories.

I am also deeply grateful for the kindness of strangers whose consequent friendship made the notion of this book possible: Aneta, Laco and Iveta for giving up the W.C. for long stretches so that I could write in there (it's the best place to concentrate!); the DeGooyer/Versteeg and Madlena families, and all the others across the continent who took me in; and to Lits Jumeaux in Leiden, Holland, for the bartending job, even though I didn't speak Dutch. And, of course, much appreciation to Kati, for the gift of the Hungarian language, and her husband, Ferenc, for his willingness to speak to me in English when I forgot.

PUBLISHER'S ACKNOWLEDGMENTS

Lonely Planet would like to thank Simon Bracken, Don George, Debra Herrmann, David McClymont, Jane Rawson, Chaman Sidhu, Naomi Springall, Marc Visnick, Vivek Waglé, Andrew Weatherill and Kieren Wheeler for their assistance in the development of this project.